1600+ Motivational Quotes By 60 Great Leaders

EDITION :   03 - (12 JANUARY 2024)

ISBN: 9798864428399 (Paperback)

ISBN: 9798864431993 (Hard Cover)

PUBLISHER :   Oyster and Pearl Publication

E-mail :   onppublications@gmail.com

Copyright © Oyster and Pearl Publication, 2023

All rights reserved. No part of this publication may be reproduced, distributed, or transmitted in any form or by any means, including photocopying, recording, or other electronic or mechanical methods, without the prior written permission of the publisher, except in the case of brief quotations embodied in critical reviews and certain other noncommercial uses permitted by copyright law. or permission requests, write to the publisher at onppublications@gmail.com

This book is a work of inspirational and motivational quotes compiled and designed by Oyster and Pearl publications. The quotes and design elements contained herein are protected by copyright law.

"1600+ Motivational Quotes By 60 Great Leaders"

MARIA RICHARDS

OYSTER AND PEARL PUBLICATION

DEDICATION

This book is dedicated to all those who believe in the power of words to inspire, uplift, and transform lives.
To my parents and teachers, whose unwavering support and encouragement fueled my passion for spreading positivity and motivation through quotes.

To the countless individuals who have shared their wisdom and words of inspiration with the world, your voices continue to make a difference.

And to you, dear reader, may these quotes serve as a source of encouragement and empowerment on your journey to success and happiness. Your constant support encourages us to build such treasure of knowledge and entertainment in the form of the books.

So, keep reading, because –

> **"**
> The only limit to what you can achieve is the limit of your knowledge. Read more, dream bigger .. and stay unstoppable.
> **"**

ACKNOWLEDGMENTS

I very pleased and excited to publish another book *"1600+ Motivational Quotes By 60 Great People"* published by Oyster and Pearl publications. I am pretty much sure that everyone of you read it will like it.

I firmly believe that quotes are like magic words that can keep us motivated, guide us through different phases of life, and help us make decisions. They have the ability to elevate our quality of life, mend broken relationships, overcome pessimism, and uplift us from failures. I can attest that 'quote' have worked wonders for me and for many others I know personally. Additionally, they can also assist and inspire those in our immediate vicinity in a myriad of ways. Motivational quotes have worked wonders for me and many others I know personally. Furthermore, they can also assist and inspire those around us in a multitude of ways.

This book will undoubtedly be a valuable resource for motivational speakers, authors, filmmakers, teachers, business professionals, and corporate individuals, just like my previous works.

Ensuring Accuracy in My Book, I've done my utmost to guarantee this book's accuracy, but attributing quotes to specific individuals can sometimes be difficult to verify. It's worth noting that attributions of quotes can sometimes be challenging to verify, and variations of the quote may exist. If you come across any mistake, quote attributed to wrong person, I encourage you to leave a comment on the marketplace (if possible) or contact me directly. I welcome any other feedback from readers and will do my best to incorporate it into the next edition.

Encouragement for Readers to Enhance Their Lives and Support Others, I urge readers to take an active role in promoting reading and improving their own quality of life. One way to do this is by rating and commenting on books through online selling platforms. Let's help others discover the joys of reading!

- Maria Richards

INDEX

1. ABRAHAM LINCOLN 11
2. ALBERT CAMUS 16
3. ALBERT EINSTEIN 22
4. ALDOUS HUXLEY 25
5. APJ ABDUL KALAM 29
6. ALEXANDER POPE 32
7. AMBROSE BIERCE 35
8. ARISTOTLE 38
9. BENJAMIN DISRAELI 41
10. BENJAMIN FRANKLIN 44
11. CONFUCIUS (KONG QUI) 47
12. DWIGHT D. EISENHOWER 50
13. EDMUND BURKE 54
14. ELBERT HUBBARD 57
15. ERIC HOFFER 61
16. EURIPIDES 64
17. FRANCIS BACON 67
18. FRANCOIS DE LA ROCHEFOUCAULD 70
19. FRIEDRICH NIETZSCHE 73
20. GEORGE BERNARD SHAW 76
21. HENRY DAVID THOREAU 79
22. HENRY WARD BEECHER 82
23. HONORE DE BALZAC 85
24. HORACE 88
25. JEAN DE LA FONTAINE 91
26. JIM ROHN 94
27. JOHANN WOLFGANG VON GOETHE 97
28. JONATHAN SWIFT 100
29. LUCIUS ANNAEUS SENECA 103

30.	MAE WEST	106
31.	MARCUS TULLIUS CICERO	109
32.	MARK TWAIN	112
33.	MASON COOLEY	117
34.	MOHANDAS (MAHATMA) GANDHI	120
35.	MOTHER TERESA	123
36.	NAPOLEON BONAPARTE	126
37.	OSCAR WILDE	130
38.	OVID	133
39.	PABLO PICASSO	136
40.	PLATO	139
41.	RALPH WALDO EMERSON	142
42.	ROBERT FROST	145
43.	SAMUEL BUTLER	148
44.	SAMUEL JOHNSON	151
45.	SOPHOCLES	154
46.	STEVEN WRIGHT	157
47.	SWAMI VIVEKANAND	160
48.	THOMAS FULLER	163
49.	THOMAS JEFFERSON	166
50.	THOMAS CARLYLE	169
51.	VICTOR HUGO	172
52.	VIRGIL	176
53.	VOLTAIRE	179
54.	WAYNE DYER	182
55.	WILL ROGERS	185
56.	WILLIAM HAZLITT	188
57.	WILLIAM JAMES	191
58.	WILLIAM SHAKESPEARE	194
59.	WINSTON CHURCHILL	197
60.	ZIG ZIGLAR	200

1. Abraham Lincoln

16th President of the United States

Nationality: American

Born: February 12, 1809,
in Hardin County, Kentucky, USA

Death: April 15, 1865,
in Washington, D.C., USA

Age: 56

Led the United States through the Civil War and abolished slavery with the Emancipation Proclamation

---

1. "Whatever you are, be a good one."

2. "Don't let personal attacks prevent you from doing what you have to do."

3. "Four score and seven years ago our fathers brought forth on this continent, a new nation, conceived in Liberty, and dedicated to the proposition that all men are created equal." (Gettysburg Address)

4. "A house divided against itself cannot stand." (House Divided Speech)

5. "The probability of a man's success increases as he goes about looking for the opportunity to help others."

6. "I have always found that mercy bears richer fruits than strict justice."

7. "No nation is fit to be a slave, and no nation is fit to have slaves."

8. "Valor is a horse; but workship is a spur."

9. "In the end, it is not the years in your life that count. It's the life in your years."

10. "It is better to be silent and be thought a fool than to speak and remove all doubt."

11. "I cannot spare the time to go to a meeting, but I will write a letter to be read at it."

12. "I believe in eating green apples." (When asked if he believed in states' rights)

13. "I don't like that man. He makes me feel like a little puppy." (About Jefferson Davis)

14. "A friend is one who has the same enemies as you."

15. "A government of the people, by the people, for the people, shall not perish from the earth." (First Inaugural Address)

16. "If I were two-faced, I'd wear this one outside." (Pointing to his backside)

17. "A penny saved is a penny earned."

18. "A drop of ink makes millions think."

19. "You cannot escape the responsibility of tomorrow by evading it today."

20. "The philosophy of the ancients has been consumed by the Moderns."

21. "Nearly all men can stand adversity, but if you want to test a man's character, give him power."

22. "The best way to predict the future is to create it."

23. "Don't believe everything you hear, and don't say everything you think."

24. "The Lord helps those who help themselves."

25. "No man is poor who has a Godly mother."

26. "Be honest and truthful and virtuous."

27. "Those who deny freedom to others deserve it not for themselves."

28. "To sin by silence when they should protest makes cowards of men."

29. "The best thing about the future is that it comes one day at a time."

30. "My concern is not whether God is on our side; my greatest concern is to be on God's side, for God is always right."

31. "Laws are made for the government of men, not the government of God."

32. "No country can long exist half slave and half free."

33. "The government which governs best governs least."

34. "Let us have faith that right makes might, and in that faith let us to our work."

35. "Public sentiment is everything. With public sentiment nothing can fail; without it nothing can succeed."

36. "I pray that I may receive, for my country and for myself, not what we deserve, but what we so greatly need."

37. "It is difficult to make men miserable when they do not allow themselves to be miserable."

38. "Those who deny freedom to others deserve it not for themselves, and cannot long retain it for themselves."

39. "Whatever you are, be a good one."

40. "With malice toward none, with charity for all, with firmness in the

right, as God gives us to see the right, let us strive on to finish the work we are in."

41. "Give me six hours to chop down a tree and I will spend the first four sharpening the axe."

42. "I learned to walk by falling down."

43. "I am a slow walker, but I never walk back."

44. "My best friend is a person who will give me a book I have not read."

45. "Speak no evil of the absent."

46. "You cannot plead poverty for not keeping faith."

****

> **SUCCESS IS NOT THE KEY OF HAPPINESS.**
> **HAPPINESS IS THE KEY OF SUCCESS.**

2. Albert Camus

Philosopher, Writer

Nationality: French (born in Algeria)

Born: November 7, 1913,
in Mondovi, French Algeria

Death: January 4, 1960,
in Villeblevin, France

Age: 46

Nobel Prize-winning author known for his existentialist philosophy and novel "The Stranger."

1. "A guilty conscience needs to confess. A work of art is a confession."

2. "A love of life can fuel an unyielding spirit, even in the face of adversity."

3. "A man's work is nothing but this slow trek to rediscover, through the detours of art, those two or three great and simple images in whose presence his heart first opened."

4. "Adversity can bring out the noblest aspects of humanity."

5. "An injustice against one innocent is a crime against humanity as a whole."

6. "Autumn is a second spring when every leaf is a flower."

7. "Belief in humanity is paramount, even without a belief in God."

8. "Beware those who preach non-judgment, for they often judge the most harshly."

9. "Don't wait for the last judgment — it takes place every day."

10. "Don't walk behind me; I may not lead. Don't walk in front of me; I may not follow. Just walk beside me and be my friend."

11. "Embrace life without hope, facing the absurdity of existence head-on."

12. "Even in the depths of winter, an invincible summer can reside within the soul."

13. "Fiction's purpose is to reveal reality, not to mirror it."

14. "Freedom is not an ideal to be pursued, but an experience to be lived."

15. "Freedom is nothing but a chance to be better."

16. "Heaven and hell are not otherworldly realms, but states of being created here on Earth."

17. "Humanity is condemned to be free, for better or worse."

18. "I should like to be able to love my country and still love justice."

19. "I would rather live my life as if there is a God and die to find out there isn't, than live my life as if there isn't and die to find out there is."

20. "I would rather not sing than sing of chains."

21. "Imagine Sisyphus happy, finding meaning in his eternal task."

22. "In an unfree world, true freedom is found in living as an act of rebellion."

23. "In the depth of winter, I finally learned that within me there lay an invincible summer."

24. "It is not your paintings I like, it is your painting."

25. "Judge a person by the questions they ask, rather than the answers they provide."

26. "Justice cannot be equated with mere order, for they are not one and the same."

27. "Life is the sum of all your choices."

28. "Living well is the ultimate revenge against those who seek to bring you down."

29. "Man is the only creature who refuses to be what he is."

30. "Prose is not about beauty, but about utility."

31. "Rebellion is the essence of existence."

32. "Revolt is the only path to self-fulfillment."

33. "Seek out challenges and create your own Everest to conquer, for true fulfillment lies in the ascent."

34. "Silence can become a profound presence within oneself."

35. "Stories should leave room for the reader to continue them in their own imagination."

36. "The absurd man finds meaning in simply existing."

37. "The artist's task is to envision what cannot be seen with the physical eye."

38. "The Mediterranean offers a lesson in living without reason."

39. "The only way to deal with this life meaningfully is to find passion in it."

40. "The purpose of a writer is to keep civilization from destroying itself."

41. "The relentless pursuit of happiness and meaning often leads to their absence."

42. "The struggle itself is enough to fill the human heart."

43. "The struggle itself toward the heights is enough to fill a man's heart. One must imagine Sisyphus happy."

44. "There is but one truly serious philosophical problem and that is suicide."

45. "To be famous, in fact, one has only to kill one's landlady."

46. "To be happy, we must not be too concerned with others."

47. "To create is to double the experience of life."

48. "To live is to embrace contradiction."

49. "To love and be loved is to bask in the warmth of the sun from all directions."

50. "Truth, like light, blinds. Falsehood, on the contrary, is a beautiful twilight that enhances every object."

51. "We used to wonder where war lived, what it was that made it so vile. And now we realize that we know where it lives... inside ourselves."

52. "When I look at my life and its secret colours, I feel like bursting into tears."

53. "When you have once seen the glow of happiness on the face of a beloved person, you know that a man can have no vocation but to awaken that light on the faces surrounding him."

54. "You know what charm is: a way of getting the answer 'yes' without having asked any clear question."

55. "You will never be able to experience everything. So, please, do poetical justice to your soul and simply experience yourself."

56. "You will never be happy if you continue to search for what happiness consists of. You will never live if you are looking for the meaning of life."

****

IF YOU WANT TO BE STRONG, FIGHT ALONE.

3. Albert Einstein

Theoretical Physicist

Nationality: Swiss-American

Born: March 14, 1879, in Ulm, Germany

Death: April 18, 1955, in Princeton, New Jersey, USA

Age: 76

Formulated the theory of relativity ($E=mc^2$) and revolutionized modern physics.

1. "Strive not to be a man of success, but rather to be a man of value."

2. "The important thing is not to stop questioning. Curiosity has its own reason for existing."

3. "Logic will get you from A to B. Imagination will get you everywhere."

4. "A person who never made a mistake never made anything."

5. "I am grateful to all those who doubted me. It made me prove them wrong."

6. "Look deep into nature, and then you will understand everything better."

7. "The definition of insanity is doing the same thing over and over again, expecting different results."

8. "Education is not the filling of a bucket, but the lighting of a fire."

9. "Peace cannot be kept by force; it can only be achieved by understanding."

10. "Imagination is more important than knowledge. Knowledge is limited. Imagination encircles the world."

11. "The only source of knowledge is experience."

12. "Try not to become a man of success, but rather try to become a man of value."

13. "The world is a dangerous place, not because of those who do evil, but because of those who do nothing about it."

14. "Science without religion is lame, religion without science is blind."

15. "We cannot solve our problems with the same kind of thinking we used when we created them."

16. "Everything should be made as simple as possible, but not simpler."

17. "The measure of intelligence is the ability to change."

18. "A ship is always safe at shore, but that is not what it is built for."

19. "The only constant in life is change."

20. "Insanity is doing the same thing over and over again and expecting different results."

21. "Weakness of attitude becomes weakness of character."

22. "The more I learn, the more I realize how much I don't know."

23. "Small is beautiful and less is more."

24. "The truth is what stands the test of experience."

25. "The most beautiful thing we can experience is the mysterious. It is the source of all true art and science."

26. "If I had an hour to solve a problem, I would spend 55 minutes thinking about the problem and the remaining 5 minutes thinking about the solutions."

27. "Education is what remains after one has forgotten what one has learned in school."

28. "Striving for success without hard work is like trying to harvest where you haven't planted."

29. "The world as we have created it is a process of our thinking. It cannot be changed without changing our thinking."

30. "It is not that I'm so smart, it's just that I stay with problems longer."

4. Aldous Huxley

Author, Philosopher

Nationality: British (English)

Born: July 26, 1894, in Godalming, Surrey, England

Death: November 22, 1963, in Los Angeles, California, USA

Age: 69

Notable for works like "Brave New World" and essays on philosophy and spirituality.

1. "After all, the greatest obstacle to discovery is not ignorance - it is the illusion of knowledge."

2. "Words can be like leaves; when they fall, they hide the roots."

3. "Experience will teach you how to be quiet. Joyful, but quiet."

4. "The more a man knows, the more he becomes aware of the limits of his own knowledge."

5. "Men seldom make mistakes, but they constantly fail to make new ones."

6. "Civilization is a race between education and catastrophe."

7. "Science without humanity is inhuman; religion without science is blind."

8. "Facts do not cease to exist because they are ignored."

9. "The more money a man has, the more he needs."

10. "Progress in the arts often results in a departure from the original intention."

11. "Love consists largely of imagination."

12. "The greatest tragedy in life is not not to have lived. It is to have lived and to look back and not be able to see anything worth living for."

13. "Sooner or later we all discover that we are our own worst enemy."

14. "The highest reward for man's toil is not what he gets for it, but what he becomes by it."

15. "All change is terrifying, even change for the better."

16. "There are things worse than death."

17. "The man who calls himself "practical" is merely the man who allows himself to be enslaved by convention."

18. "The future is not a gift. It is an achievement."

19. "What a dreadful mistake it is to think that happiness consists in anything but the present moment!"

20. "Knowledge that does not enlighten the soul is sterile knowledge."

21. "To say what one thinks, without regard for consequences, is a privilege of the rich."

22. "The secret of genius is to carry the spirit of childhood into maturity - which means never to lose that love of wonder which is the source of creative imagination."

23. "There is only one corner of the universe you are sure of improving, and that is your own self."

24. "Experience is not what happens to a man; it is what a man does with what happens to him."

25. "Facts themselves don't speak until someone gives them a voice."

26. "Words don't mean a thing. It's what they do to you that matters."

27. "What happens when a civilization begins to lose its sense of sin? Why, it loses its sense of proportion, of course."

28. "It is the business of art to deal with the impossible."

29. "There is only one final victory, and that is the victory over oneself."

30. "True religion is the discovery of that in us which can never be hurt, never be defeated."

****

5. APJ Abdul Kalam

Scientist, President of India

Nationality: Indian

Born: October 15, 1931, in Rameswaram, Tamil Nadu, India.

Death: July 27, 2015, in Shillong, India

Age: 83

Renowned Indian scientist and the 11th President of India, known as the "People's President" and for his contributions to space and missile technology.

1. Dream, dream, dream. Dreams transform into thoughts, and thoughts result in action.

2. You have to dream before your dreams can come true.

3. Don't take rest after your first victory because if you fail in the second, more lips are waiting to say that your first victory was just luck.

4. If you want to shine like a sun, first burn like a sun.

5. All of us do not have equal talent, but all of us should have an equal opportunity to develop our talents.

6. Failure will never overtake me if my determination to succeed is strong enough.

7. In life, you need either inspiration or desperation.

8. To succeed in your mission, you must have single-minded devotion to your goal.

9. Great dreams of great dreamers are always transcended.

10. You should not give up and we should not allow the problem to defeat us.

11. Man needs his difficulties because they are necessary to enjoy success.

12. Climbing to the top demands strength, whether it is to the top of Mount Everest or to the top of your career.

13. Excellence is a continuous process and not an accident.

14. Thinking is the capital, enterprise is the way, hard work is the solution.

15. Teaching is a very noble profession that shapes the character, caliber, and future of an individual.

16. Let us sacrifice our today so that our children can have a better tomorrow.

17. Learning gives creativity. Creativity leads to thinking. Thinking

provides knowledge. Knowledge makes you great.

18. One best book is equal to a hundred good friends, but one good friend is equal to a library.

19. The best brains of the nation may be found on the last benches of the classroom.

20. Small aim is a crime; have great aim.

****

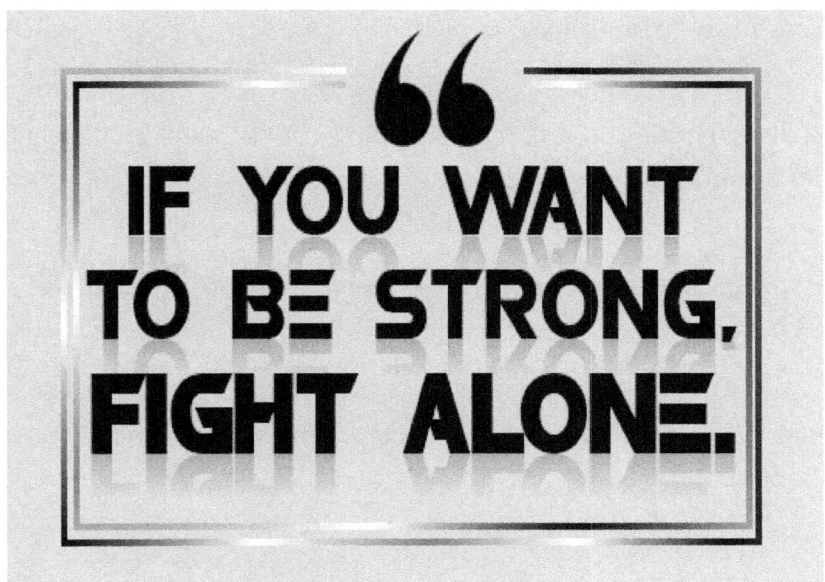

6. Alexander Pope

Poet, Satirist

Nationality: British (English)

Born: May 21, 1688, in London, England

Death: May 30, 1744, in Twickenham, England

Age: 56

Renowned for his satirical poems and "The Rape of the Lock."

1. "Fools rush in where angels fear to tread."

2. "To err is human; to forgive, divine."

3. "A little learning is a dangerous thing; Drink deep, or taste not the Pierian spring."

4. "Hope springs eternal in the human breast: Man never is, but always to be blest."

5. "Blessed is the man who expects nothing, for he shall never be disappointed."

6. "Be not the first by whom the new are tried, Nor yet the last to lay the old aside."

7. "Honor and shame from no condition rise; Act well your part: there all the honor lies."

8. "For forms of Government let fools contest; Whate'er is best administered is best."

9. "What dire offense from amorous causes springs, What mighty contests rise from trivial things!"

10. "Know then thyself, presume not God to scan; The proper study of mankind is Man."

11. "Oh thoughtless mortals! ever blind to fate, Too soon dejected, and too soon elate."

12. "Praise undeserved is satire in disguise."

13. "Charm strikes the sight, but merit wins the soul."

14. "All nature is but art unknown to thee."

15. "'Tis education forms the common mind; Just as the twig is bent the tree's inclined."

16. "The proper study of mankind is Man."

17. "Hope springs eternal in the human breast."

18. "A little learning is a dangerous thing."

19. "The greatest foe to truth is often more than lies; Tis prejudice and custom, a cloud it spreads."

20. "Know then thyself, presume not God to scan."

21. "Fear not the anger of the wise and brave; Man will but blush to give the wretch a grave."

22. "What makes all doctrines plain and clear? What, but a head and heart well-paired?"

23. "If to her share some female errors fall, Look on her face, and you'll forget 'em all."

24. "Let such teach others who themselves excel, And censure freely who have written well."

25. "But when to mischief mortals bend their will, How soon they find fit instruments of ill!"

26. "Who in the stream a falling star surveys, May count as many shining drops as rays."

****

7. Ambrose Bierce

Author, Journalist

Nationality: American

Born: June 24, 1842, in Horse Cave Creek, Ohio, USA

Death: After 1914 (disappeared during the Mexican Revolution)

Age: unknown

Notable for his short stories and sardonic wit, including "The Devil's Dictionary."

1. "War is God's way of teaching American's geography."

2. "Laughter is the chloroform of the soul."

3. "Cynicism is an iron tonic; it braces the mind for disappointment."

4. "The man who marries for money deserves neither the woman nor the money."

5. "Patriotism, n. The willingness to kill and be killed for trivial reasons."

6. "A diplomat is a man who can lie convincingly."

7. "Happiness is a butterfly which, when pursued, is always just beyond your grasp, but which, if you sit down quietly, may alight upon you."

8. "Silence is a confession when speech would be a defense."

9. "Courage is a quality of mind which enables a man to face the dangers of life with firmness."

10. "A lie is an abomination before the Lord, but after all the Lord isn't very bright."

11. "The hardest thing to understand in the world is the income tax."

12. "Love is a burning coal upon the tip of which a fool gets blistered."

13. "I have never found the pursuit of truth to be an aid to optimism."

14. "A pessimist sees the glass as half empty. An optimist sees it as half full. A pragmatist pours himself another drink."

15. "A bicycle built for two is not necessarily made for love, but sometimes it's the nearest thing to it."

16. "To love one's country requires some art; to hate it is as natural as falling downstairs."

17. "The only difference between a good lawyer and a bad one is the price."

18. "The American is the most religious of all civilized peoples, and consequently the most barbarous."

19. "An optimist is a person who sees a way through everything; a pessimist is a person who sees everything through."

20. "The mind is everything. What you think you become."

21. "Experience: A comb which nature gives to men when they are bald."

22. "Truth is stranger than fiction, but it is because fiction has to make sense."

23. "A friend is one who knows all about you and still likes you."

24. "There are no secrets the dead cannot keep."

25. "The art of deception is one in which women excel."

26. "The art of writing is the art of applying the eraser."

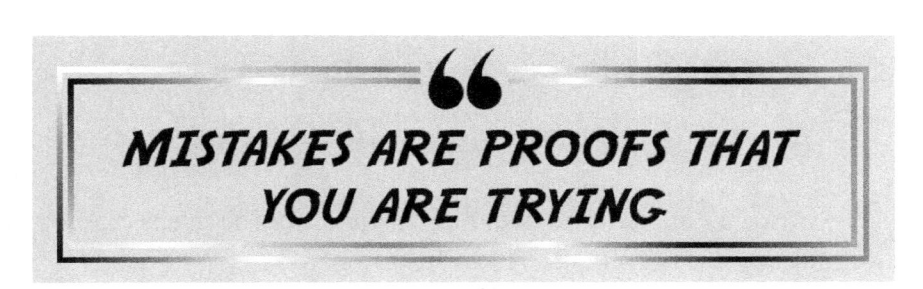

****

> **MISTAKES ARE PROOFS THAT YOU ARE TRYING**

8. Aristotle

Philosopher, Scientist

Nationality: Greek

Born: 384 BC, in Stagira, Greece

Death: 322 BC, in Euboea, Greece

Age: 62 (approx.)

Influential ancient Greek philosopher and student of Plato, known for his contributions to ethics, politics, and natural science.

1. "The only true wealth is knowledge, and the only true education is in learning something useful."

2. "Happiness is the meaning and the purpose of life, the whole aim and end of human existence."

3. "It is the mark of an educated mind to be able to entertain a thought without accepting it."

4. "We are what we repeatedly do. Excellence, then, is not an act but a habit."

5. "There is only one way to avoid criticism: do nothing, say nothing, be nothing."

6. "For man is by nature a political animal."

7. "The aim of education is to learn to think rightly, and to act rightly."

8. "Friendship is a single soul dwelling in two bodies."

9. "The unexamined life is not worth living."

10. "Pleasure in the job puts perfection in the work. Therefore, only by working can you achieve perfection."

11. "All men by nature desire knowledge."

12. "It is more difficult to be a friend than an enemy."

13. "The greatest good is not to enjoy the best, but to be the best you can be."

14. "Poverty is the parent of crime."

15. "Courage is the virtue that knows how to fear what one should fear and how not to fear what one should not fear."

16. "The good are only happy in the company of the good."

17. "Wonder is the beginning of philosophy."

18. "In every friendship there is an element of equality."

19. "Time is the most precious of all possessions."

20. "Silence is a true friend who never betrays."

21. "He who cannot be silent cannot speak properly."

22. "To love means to will the good of the other."

23. "The only way to make a man good is to treat him as if he already were."

24. "Man alone among the animals has the sense of good and evil."

25. "Education is an ornament in prosperity and a refuge in adversity."

26. "The more you praise and extol a thing, the more you strip it of its real value."

27. "Patience is bitter, but its fruit is sweet."

28. "A friend to all is a friend to none."

*****

9. Benjamin Disraeli

British Prime Minister

Nationality: British (English)

Born: December 21, 1804, in London, England

Death: April 19, 1881, in London, England

Age: 76

Served as Prime Minister twice and played a key role in the expansion of the British Empire.

1. "The greatest good is not to enjoy the best, but to be the best you can be."

2. "The greatest happiness is to have the conviction of being loved for yourself alone."

3. "A man who never makes mistakes never makes anything."

4. "The greatest gift a father can give to his son is a mother who loves him."

5. "The secret of success is constancy of purpose."

6. "A pessimist sees the difficulty in every opportunity; an optimist sees the opportunity in every difficulty."

7. "Justice is truth in action."

8. "Power tends to corrupt, and absolute power corrupts absolutely."

9. "There is no education like hardship."

10. "The greatest mistake you can make is to be continuously afraid you will make one."

11. "A nation should be governed for the prosperity of the people and not for the vanity of the rulers."

12. "The greatest pleasure in life is to talk about yourself."

13. "Never apologize for burning bridges. People who cross them deserve to be isolated."

14. "The greatest secrets are always the simplest."

15. "A conservative is a man who is afraid to walk backwards but who remembers where he has been."

16. "Youth is the time for making mistakes; middle age is the time for living with them."

17. "The wisest of all men is he who knows himself to be foolish."

18. "A man is not old until regrets take the place of dreams."

19. "Success is a two-headed monster; the one head devours the present, the other the future."

20. "Nurture your mind with great thoughts. To believe in the heroic makes heroes."

21. "You can complain because roses have thorns, or you can rejoice because thorns have roses."

22. "The greatest pleasure in life is to watch your enemies being roasted."

23. "The reason why so few men understand life is because they understand it only from their own point of view."

24. "There are two kinds of people: those who achieve and those who make excuses."

25. "Ignorance is a perpetual mistress that he loves and prizes."

26. "The truth is rarely pure and never simple."

27. "A man's wisdom is often no more than the accumulation of his memories."

****

10. Benjamin Franklin

Inventor, Statesman

Nationality: American

Born: January 17, 1706,
in Boston, Massachusetts, USA

Death: April 17, 1790,
in Philadelphia, Pennsylvania, USA

Age: 84

Renowned polymath known for his experiments with electricity and contributions to American independence.

1. "An investment in knowledge pays the best interest."

2. "Early to bed and early to rise makes a man healthy, wealthy, and wise."

3. "Three may keep a secret, if two of them are dead."

4. "Honesty is the best policy."

5. "Well done is better than well said."

6. "There are three things extremely hard: steel, a diamond, and to know oneself."

7. "By failing to prepare, you are preparing to fail."

8. "He that cannot forgive others, breaks the bridge over which he must himself pass."

9. "For every minute spent organizing, an hour is earned."

10. "Beware of little expenses; a small leak will sink a great ship."

11. "The only way to do great work is to love what you do."

12. "Guests, like fish, begin to stink after three days."

13. "Silence is often the true sign of friendship."

14. "Those who would give up essential liberty to purchase a little temporary safety, deserve neither liberty nor safety."

15. "Never do today what you can put off until tomorrow."

16. "An ounce of prevention is worth a pound of cure."

17. "Waste not, want not."

18. "Love your enemies, for they tell you your faults."

19. "Three removes are as bad as a fire."

20. "Time is money."

21. "A penny saved is a penny earned."

22. "There is no such thing as a free lunch."

23. "Experience keeps a dear school, but fools will learn in no other."

24. "If you would have your servant honest, pay him well."

25. "Justice is blind."

26. "Necessity is the mother of invention."

27. "He that lives upon hopes will die fasting."

28. "Well begun is half done."

29. "The way to wealth is as plain as the way to market."

30. "God helps those who help themselves."

****

11. Confucius (Kong Qui)

Philosopher, Teacher

Nationality: Chinese (Ancient Chinese)

Born: 551 BC, in Zou, Lu State (now Qufu, Shandong Province, China)

Death: 479 BC, in Lu State (now Qufu, Shandong Province, China)

Age: 72

Founder of Confucianism, a major school of thought in Chinese philosophy.

1. "Before you embark on a journey of revenge, dig two graves."

2. "Wherever you go, go with all your heart."

3. "Real knowledge is to know the extent of one's ignorance."

4. "It does not matter how slowly you go as long as you do not stop."

5. "Our greatest glory is not in never falling, but in rising every time we fall."

6. "Silence is a true friend who never betrays."

7. "To see what is right and not do it is want of courage."

8. "Choose a job you love, and you will never have to work a day in your life."

9. "The superior man is modest in his speech, but exceeds in his actions."

10. "Do not impose on others what you yourself do not desire."

11. "The journey of a thousand miles begins with a single step."

12. "The man who asks a question is a fool for a minute, the man who does not ask is a fool for life."

13. "Respect yourself and others will respect you."

14. "It is better to light one small candle than to curse the darkness."

15. "The superior man is distressed by the limitations of his abilities; he is not distressed by the fact that men do not recognize the ability that he has."

16. "To be wronged is nothing unless you continue to remember it."

17. "The journey of a thousand miles begins with a single step."

18. "Three armies may be readily routed, but the nation that governs its own moral force is invincible."

19. "It is not possible to serve two masters."

20. "He who learns but does not think, is lost. He who thinks but does not learn, is in great danger."

21. "Everything has beauty, but not everyone sees it."

22. "Worry not that no one knows you; seek to be worth knowing."

23. "The superior man is distressed by the limitations of his abilities; he is not distressed by the fact that men do not recognize the ability that he has."

24. "The superior man is modest in his speech, but exceeds in his actions."

25. "To be wronged is nothing unless you continue to remember it."

****

> **YOUR WORDS STARTS TO LOSE VALUE, WHEN YOUR ACTION DON'T MATCH**

12. Dwight D. Eisenhower

34th U.S. President

Nationality: American

Born: October 14, 1890, in Denison, Texas, USA

Death: March 28, 1969, in Washington, D.C., USA

Age: 78

Supreme Allied Commander in World War II and U.S. President during the Cold War era.

1. "A pessimist sees the difficulty in every opportunity; an optimist sees the opportunity in every difficulty."

2. "Leadership is the art of getting someone else to do something you want done because he wants to do it."

3. "Don't tell people how to do things, tell them what to do and let them surprise you with their results."

4. "Plans are worthless, but planning is everything."

5. "I have learned that as long as one has confidence in one's powers, no matter how long the odds are, you'll have the strength to succeed."

6. "Take the initiative! You can't swim by sitting on the bank."

7. "Get the best information you can. Then make the best decision you can. The results will probably be bad anyway. Don't cry over spilt milk, but do learn from your mistakes."

8. "A nation reveals itself not in how it treats its highest citizens, but in how it treats its most vulnerable ones."

9. "Every gun that is made, every warship launched, every rocket fired signifies in the final sense a theft from the people who hunger and go unclothed."

10. "Peace is not just the absence of war, it's the presence of justice."

11. "The greatest danger for most of us is not that our aim is too high and we miss it, but that it is too low and we reach it."

12. "If you are going to plan for a year, plant rice. If you are going to plan for ten years, plant trees. If you are going to plan for a hundred years, educate people."

13. "Politics ought to be the part-time profession of every citizen who wants to govern according to his conscience."

14. "A friend in need is a friend indeed, but an enemy in need is a business opportunity."

15. "The United States cannot escape its responsibility."

16. "Humility is not thinking low of yourself, it's thinking of yourself less."

17. "The difference between ordinary and extraordinary is that little extra."

18. "The important thing is not to stop questioning. Curiosity has its own reason for existing."

19. "The supreme function of leadership is to change and predict. If you wait for events, you will find yourself only picking up the pieces."

20. "The trouble with dictators is that they have too many advisers who say 'yes.'"

21. "A date at Carnegie Hall is finer than a week at the fair."

22. "Never apologize for being successful."

23. "There is nothing worse than a battle fought halfway through."

24. "Every problem is an opportunity in disguise."

25. "Leadership is the art of persuading people to do what you want done because they want to do it."

26. "A leader leads by example."

27. "The best place to hide a secret is in plain sight."

28. "You have to give the people hope. Hope in their future and hope in themselves."

****

THE BEST PROJECT YOU'LL EVER WORK ON IS YOU.

13. Edmund Burke

Philosopher, Statesman

Nationality: Irish (later British)

Born: January 12, 1729, in Dublin, Ireland

Death: July 9, 1797, in Beaconsfield, England

Age: 68

Influential political philosopher and Member of Parliament, known for his support of conservatism.

1. "The only thing necessary for the triumph of evil is for good men to do nothing."

2. "People will never look for justice where they do not see mercy."

3. "Those who would give up essential liberty to purchase a little temporary safety, deserve neither liberty nor safety."

4. "Applaud the virtues of those who differ from you most; condemn the vices of those who think exactly like you."

5. "The greater part of the miseries and evils which men suffer, come from their dwelling in conceit, instead of confiding in wisdom and experience."

6. "Society cannot exist unless a controlling power upon will and

appetite be placed somewhere, and the law is that power."

7. "A state without the means of some change is without the means of its own conservation."

8. "To a great part, the faults of statesmen are the faults of the public."

9. "All that is necessary for the triumph of evil is for good men to do nothing."

10. "The education of the mind should be adjusted to the education of the heart."

11. "The age is always busy to tell you it is more prudent than those that went before it, and wiser than all that are to come after it."

12. "The greatest calamity that can fall upon any nation is the calamity of having a single standard of opinion."

13. "The laws of trade and the laws of nations are not, like the laws of nature, fixed and immutable."

14. "The law is not the will of any individual; it is the wisdom of the whole."

15. "The foundation of every state, the corner-stone of all good laws, is public opinion."

16. "A common interest, not a common opinion, makes the cement of the nation."

17. "When anger throws aside the reins, discretion loses its hold."

18. "The revolution of the seasons is the calendar of nature, and the revolutions of empires the calendar of time."

19. "He that wrestles with the laws of nature, is certain of being thrown."

20. "The greater the power, the more dangerous the abuse."

21. "When anger throws aside the reins, discretion loses its hold."

22. "Education is the bread of life, and if a man is not fed with it, he is starved."

23. "The foundation of every state, the corner-stone of all good laws, is public opinion."

****

14. Elbert Hubbard

Writer, Philosopher

Nationality: American

Born: June 19, 1856,
in Bloomington, Illinois, USA

Death: May 7, 1915
(in the sinking of the RMS Lusitania, Irish Sea)

Age: 58

Founder of the Roycroft artisan community and author of the essay "A Message to Garcia."

1. "Do your work with intensity and interest. One kind word can change a life."

2. "A little neglect may kill your finest friendships, and a little thoughtlessness turn love to ashes."

3. "The greatest mistake in the world is to be continually afraid you will make one."

4. "A man's greatness lies not in how much wealth he acquires, but in his character and the positive influence he leaves upon others."

5. "The greatest remedy for those who are afraid, lonely or unhappy is to go outside, somewhere where they can be quite alone with the heavens, nature and God."

6. "He who knows how to talk to any one on the street is already a good salesman; he who knows how to talk to any one in the street and make him buy something, is a salesman indeed."

7. "All good things come hard; that's why they're good."

8. "The greatest compliment that was ever paid me was when someone asked me what I thought about the new fashions and I answered, 'I don't know.'"

9. "To avoid criticism do nothing, say nothing, be nothing."

10. "The difference between a successful person and others is not a lack of strength, not a lack of knowledge, but rather a lack of will."

11. "The greatest happiness in life is the conviction that you are loved for yourself, not for any mask you wear or role you play."

12. "The greatest glory in living lies not in never falling, but in rising every time we fall."

13. "Never criticize, condemn or complain. If you are unhappy with anything, change it. If you cannot change it, change your attitude."

14. "The only person who is educated is the one who has learned how to learn and change."

15. "The best way to predict your future is to create it."

16. "The things a man has are not important; the important thing is what he is."

17. "Do not take life too seriously. You cannot win against it."

18. "The only way to do great work is to love what you do."

19. "He that cannot forgive others, breaks the bridge over which he must himself pass."

20. "You are not paid for having a job. You are paid for the value you bring to the job."

21. "The greatest thing in the world is to know how to belong to oneself."

22. "Life is a journey, not a destination."

23. "The only person you are destined to become is the person you decide to be."

24. "Doubt kills more dreams than failure ever will."

25. "It is not the mountain we conquer but ourselves."

26. "The only way to make a man good is to treat him as if he already were."

27. "The greatest weakness of all is fear."

28. "The only thing that wears out faster than a smile is a frown."

29. "The only way to make a friend is to be one."

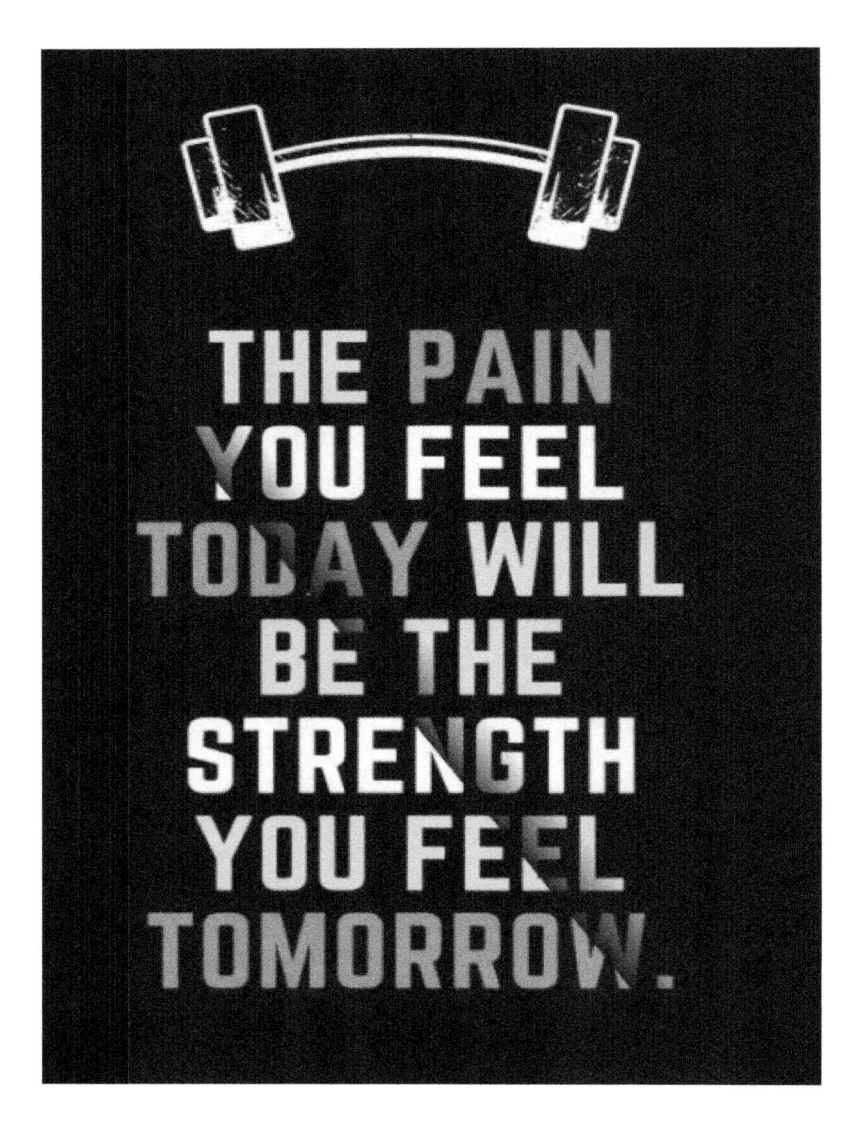

****

15. Eric Hoffer

Philosopher, Author

Nationality: American

Born: July 25, 1902,
in New York City, New York, USA

Death: May 21, 1983,
in San Francisco, California, USA
Age: 80

Wrote "The True Believer," an analysis of mass movements and fanaticism.

1. "Man is most uneasy when he is at rest."

2. "In a great crisis, men often act better than their normal standards because they find in themselves more than ordinary resources."

3. "Hope is a good breakfast, but it is a bad supper."

4. "The trouble with most of us is that we would like to be somebody else."

5. "The mass of men always prefers the man of action to the man of words."

6. "The reformer is almost invariably a conservative when put upon his own."

7. "The worst form of inequality is to try to make unequal things equal."

8. "A fanatic is one who can't change his mind and won't change the subject."

9. "The greater the security, the greater the boredom."

10. "The strongest and sweetest songs yet remain to be sung."

11. "The truest test of a civilization is in the way it treats its weak and helpless."

12. "Nothing is so intolerable as prosperity without an outlet for action."

13. "No change or upheaval is good or bad in itself. It is the direction it takes and the spirit that animates it that determines its value."

14. "Men who feel guilty are often drawn to causes that promise to wipe out guilt by collective vengeance."

15. "Mass movements arise out of the common experience of frustration rather than out of any common ideology."

16. "Enthusiasm is the mother of mischief, but also the father of achievement."

17. "There are as many ways of looking at life as there are people in the world."

18. "To learn from experience one must first have the experience."

19. "The great masses of people are more moved by feelings than by reason."

20. "Progress often results from disasters."

21. "The highest form of self-esteem is based on merit, not on praise."

22. "The worst loneliness is to not be comfortable with yourself."

23. "The future belongs to those who believe in the beauty of their dreams."

24. "The measure of a man is not how high he climbs but how he bounces when he hits the bottom."

25. "Fanaticism is the result of intellectual laziness."

26. "The revolution starts first in the hearts and minds of men."

27. "The most dangerous men are not the ignorant, but those who are ignorant and know it."

28. "The man who has no imagination has no wings."

29. "The more a man has, the more he wants."

16. Euripides

Playwright, Tragedian

Nationality: Ancient Greek

Born: 480 BC, in Salamis, Ancient Athens (now Cyprus)

Death: 406 BC, in Pella, Macedon (now Greece)

Age: 74

Renowned ancient Greek playwright known for tragedies like "Medea."

1. "Silence is a true friend who never betrays."

2. "The tongue is a powerful thing, for it can bring both joy and grief."

3. "Whoever knows the art of loving, knows the art of dying."

4. "He that is wounded by love, loves still."

5. "The tongue can bring both ruin and salvation."

6. "Even silence can betray the heart."

7. "Of all evils the worst is to leave behind you undone those things which you ought to have done."

8. "There is no fool like an old fool."

9. "Love conquers all things, even the impossible."

10. "The gods punish those whom they wish to destroy."

11. "Fortune laughs at fools."

12. "No man should be called happy until after he is dead."

13. "The tongue is most dangerous and worst weapon you can own."

14. "Love is a deep ocean; no man knows its depths."

15. "Wine consoles the wise, not the foolish."

16. "Hope is the dream of a waking man."

17. "It is better to die well than to live badly."

18. "Those who are silent suffer."

19. "The greatest evil is to see and not understand."

20. "Wine, women, and song, distract men from thoughts of war."

21. "Speech is silver, silence is golden."

22. "Those whom the gods love die young."

23. "The greater the sinner, the greater the saint."

24. "It is base to envy even a god."

25. "Beauty fades, but virtue blooms."

26. "He who hesitates is lost."

27. "A friend in need is a friend indeed."

28. "Silence is a true friend who never betrays."

29. "The truth is often hidden in lies."

****

> BE NOT AFRAID OF GROWING SLOWLY, AFRAID ONLY BY NOT STARTING OR STANDING STILL.

17. Francis Bacon

Philosopher, Statesman

Nationality: British (English)

Born: January 22, 1561, in London, England

Death: April 9, 1626, in Highgate, London, England

Age: 65

Known as the "father of empiricism" and for his contributions to the scientific method.

1. "Knowledge is power."

2. "The greatest friend of truth is Time, her greatest enemy Prejudice, and her constant companion Humility."

3. "Hope is a good breakfast, but it is a bad supper."

4. "Reading maketh a full man; conference a ready man; and writing an exact man."

5. "Anything can be achieved if it is first dreamt."

6. "The only way to make progress is to try."

7. "Wisely and slowly. They stumble that run fast."

8. "Whoso discovers himself to be a master of speech will find himself a master of action."

9. "A dwarf standing on the shoulders of a giant can see farther than the giant himself."

10. "Silence is the true ornament of speech."

11. "Studies serve for delight, for ornament, and for ability."

12. "No man's knowledge can reach his own conspiracies."

13. "A discontented mind cannot choose what is best."

14. "He that cannot conceive deformity and form it as well as beauty, hath no place amongst the true masters."

15. "Every man's fortune hangs from the uncertainty of a die."

16. "Money is a great matter, and the want of it the root of all evil."

17. "Custom, that most blind tyrant of all."

18. "A friend is one soul dwelling in two bodies."

19. "The aim of science is to find unity in diversity."

20. "Time is the wisest counselor of all."

21. "Beauty is nature's color-gift to the world."

22. "Observation is the foundation of all true knowledge."

23. "Travel, in the younger sort, is a part of education; in the elder, a part of experience."

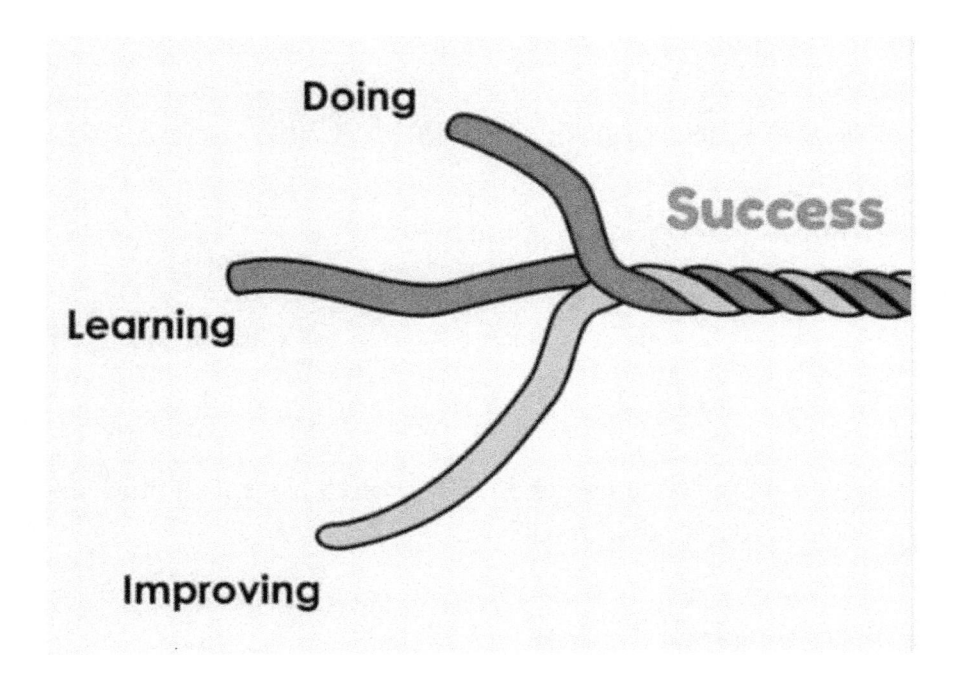

****

18. Francois De La Rochefoucauld

Writer, Moralist

Nationality: French

Born: September 15, 1613, in Paris, France

Death: March 17, 1680, in Paris, France

Age: 66

Famous for his "Maxims," a collection of witty and insightful aphorisms.

1. "We are more concerned about our reputation with other people than about our conscience with ourselves."

2. "Hypocrisy is the homage that vice pays to virtue."

3. "To refuse praise is to seek praise twice."

4. "True love is like ghosts, which everyone talks about and few have seen."

5. "We are more concerned about our shortcomings with other people than about our vices with ourselves."

6. "The only constant is change."

7. "The greatest part of our happiness depends on our dispositions, not our circumstances."

8. "We promise according to our hopes, and perform according to our fears."

9. "Few people have the wisdom to prefer the criticism that would do them good, to the praise that deceives them."

10. "We often forgive those who bore us, but we cannot forgive those whom we bore."

11. "Our virtues are most often disguised vices."

12. "In jealousy, there is more of self-love than love."

13. "It is easier to be wise for others than for ourselves."

14. "We always love those who admire us, but we do not always love those whom we admire."

15. "The defects of the mind, like those of the face, grow worse with age."

16. "In the misfortunes of our best friends, we always find something that is not displeasing to us."

17. "To succeed in the world, we do everything we can to appear successful already."

18. "The praise that comes from love does not make us vain, but more

humble."

19. "The love of justice is simply, in the majority of men, the fear of suffering injustice."

20. "Our repentance is not so much sorrow for the ill we have done as fear of the ill that may happen to us in consequence."

21. "It is with an old love as it is with old age, a man lives to all the miseries but is dead to all the pleasures."

22. "A refusal of praise is a desire to be praised twice."

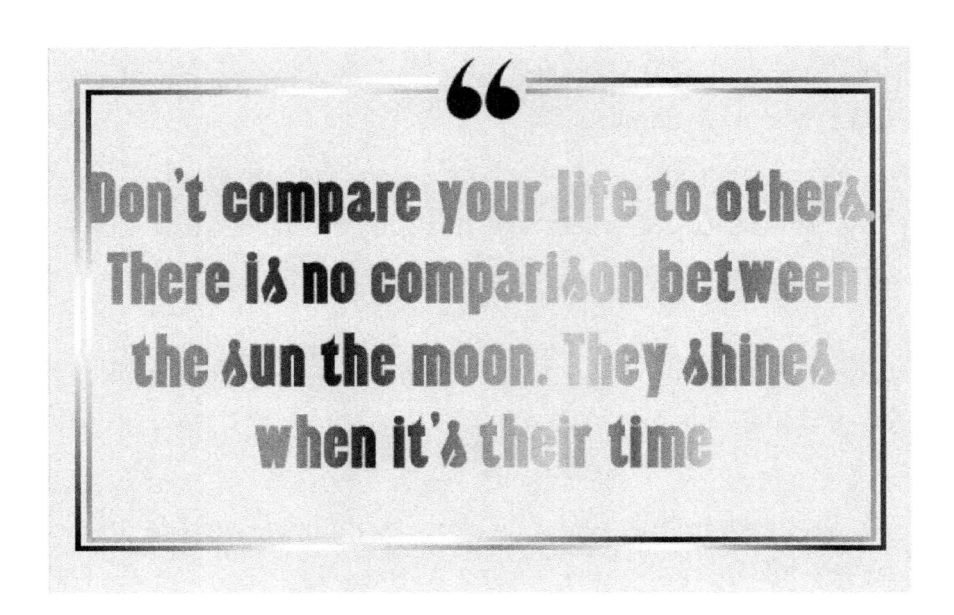

****

> " Don't compare your life to others. There is no comparison between the sun the moon. They shines when it's their time

19. Friedrich Nietzsche

Philosopher, Writer

Nationality: German

Born: October 15, 1844, in Röcken, Germany

Death: August 25, 1900, in Weimar, Germany

Age: 55

Known for his works on existentialism and the concept of the "Übermensch" (Overman)

1. "He who has a why to live can bear almost any how."

2. "What does not kill me, makes me stronger."

3. "Become the master of your fate, the captain of your soul."

4. "The only true voyage of discovery is not in seeking new landscapes, but in having new eyes."

5. "There are no moral phenomena, only moral interpretations of phenomena."

6. "Beware of those who come bearing gifts."

7. "The greatest danger for most of us is not that our aim is too high and we miss it, but that it is too low and we reach it."

8. "Man is a rope, tied at one end to the animal and at the other to the superhuman."

9. "The individual has always been sacrificed to the community, but the time has come to sacrifice the community to the individual."

10. "Whoever fights monsters should see to it that in the process he does not become a monster himself."

11. "You have to give the people hope. Hope in their future and hope in themselves."

12. "Without music, life would be a mistake."

13. "The coldest hearts do not freeze, they burn."

14. "What is done out of love always takes place beyond good and evil."

15. "He who laughs last laughs best."

16. "Fall in love with your career. It deserves the whole of your heart."

17. "One must learn to love oneself with a wholesome and reverent heart, so that one can be a mirror to one's neighbor."

18. "The truth is rarely pure and never simple."

19. "Whoever seeks greatness should forget greatness."

20. "There are two kinds of people: those who achieve and those who make excuses."

21. "The superior man is distressed by the limitations of his abilities; he is not distressed by the fact that men do not recognize the ability that he has."

22. "Beware of pity, for it is often the cloak for concealed arrogance and the desire to feel superior."

23. "The will to power, that is the ultimate motive behind life."

****

> **If you get tired, Learn to rest, not to quit.**

20. George Bernard Shaw

Playwright, Critic

Nationality: Irish (later British)

Born: July 26, 1856, in Dublin, Ireland

Death: November 2, 1950, in Ayot St Lawrence, Hertfordshire, England

Age: 94

Prolific playwright and critic, awarded the Nobel Prize in Literature in 1925

1. "The reasonable man adapts himself to the world; the unreasonable one persists in trying to adapt the world to himself. Therefore all progress depends on the unreasonable man."

2. "Don't worry about the result, let the play be all you are capable of giving. The rest is in the hands of fate."

3. "I like nonsense, it wakes up the brain cells. I do not say everything nonsense. In fact, most of the time I am wrong."

4. "The only way to deal with unreasonable people is to remove yourself from the situation. If you cannot walk away, set a boundary and enforce it."

5. "We learn from failure, not from success!"

6. "I write like I talk. Talking is my trade. I haven't been given this gift of articulate speech just to keep it under a bushel."

7. "The time that is lost in hesitation is more than enough to succeed."

8. "The old believe everything; the middle-aged suspect everything; the young know everything."

9. "Never underestimate the power of a simple, clean truth."

10. "The more a man has, the more he wants."

11. "Intellectuals love complexity. I'm no damn intellectual."

12. "Liberty without wisdom is a wild beast."

13. "A house is not a home unless it contains food and fire for the mind as well as the body."

14. "All professions are conspiracies against the laity."

15. "The two things most dangerous to a writer are alcohol and self-belief."

16. "A man's errors are more instructive than his achievements."

17. "The English never do anything until they have to."

18. "Progress is only possible if we venture beyond the safe paths where experience can guide us."

19. "It is the mark of a truly intelligent person to be able to entertain a thought without accepting it."

20. "Don't walk in front of me, I may not follow. Don't walk behind me, I may not lead. Walk beside me, and be my friend."

21. "The problem with idiots is that they are always thinking up new ways to be idiots."

22. "Some people see things as they are and ask why. I dream things that never were and ask why not."

23. "The only person on earth who is completely unsympathetic is one's self."

24. "All the world's a stage, and all the men and women merely players."

****

> Investing in yourself is the investment you will ever make. It will not only improve your life, it will improve the lives of all those around you

21. Henry David Thoreau

Philosopher, Author

Nationality: American

Born: July 12, 1817,
in Concord, Massachusetts, USA

Death: May 6, 1862,
in Concord, Massachusetts, USA

Age: 44

Author of "Walden" and an advocate for simplicity and nature

1. "I went to the woods because I wished to live deliberately, to front only the essential facts of life, and see if I could not learn what it had to teach, and not, when I came to die, discover that I had not lived." (Walden)

2. "Most of the luxuries, and many of the so-called comforts of life, are not only not indispensable, but positive hindrances to the elevation of mankind." (Walden)

3. "Go confidently in the direction of your dreams. Live the life you have imagined."

4. "As you simplify your life, the laws of the universe will become clearer."

5. "In wildness is the preservation of the world."

6. "Civil disobedience is not a protest. It is the refusal to cooperate with an evil government. It is not to say 'no' but to say 'yes' to something higher."

7. "Civil disobedience is not a perfect weapon. Neither is it a weapon for the weak and cowardly. It is the weapon of the brave."

8. "If a man does not keep pace with his companions, perhaps it is because he hears a different drummer."

9. "The greatest glory in living lies not in never falling, but in rising every time we fall."

10. "I learned this, at least, by my experiment; that if one advances confidently in the direction of his dreams, and endeavors to live the life which he has imagined, he will meet with a success unexpected in common hours."

11. "I am not interested in conservation. I am interested in wildness."

12. "What I have to say is not so important as the fact that I say it."

13. "The mass of men lead lives of quiet desperation."

14. "The price of anything is the amount of life you exchange for it."

15. "Men are not so bad as they seem, nor so good as they pretend."

16. "If the only prayer you say in your life is thank you, that would suffice."

17. "The fault is not in the stars, but in ourselves, that we are underlings."

18. "As a single gentle rain makes the desert bloom, so does a single thought of love make the soul blossom."

19. "The world is not interested in conformity. It rewards originality."

20. "I believe that there is a soul under the ribs of each and every one of us."

21. "Caution is the sister of fear."

22. "I believe that every one is guilty of some self-imposed blindness."

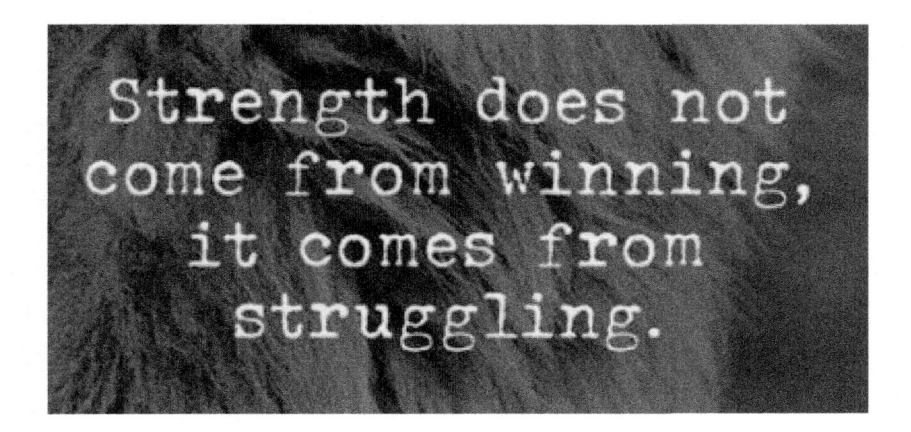

****

> Strength does not come from winning, it comes from struggling.

22. Henry Ward Beecher

Minister, Abolitionist

Nationality: American

Born: June 24, 1813, in Litchfield, Connecticut, USA

Death: March 8, 1887, in Brooklyn, New York, USA

Age: 73

Prominent clergyman and social reformer, known for his anti-slavery views.

1. "Opportunity knocks once in a lifetime. But, most people mistake it for knocking."

2. "Every life, no matter how long and happy, is but a moment in eternity."

3. "Doubt kills more dreams than failure ever will."

4. "A smile is the universal language of kindness."

5. "Gratitude is not a duty but an opportunity."

6. "The two most important days in your life are the day you are born and the day you find out why."

7. "The highest result of education is tolerance."

8. "Sow a thought, reap an action; sow an action, reap a habit; sow a habit, reap a character; sow a character, reap a destiny."

9. "Keep your face to the sunshine and you cannot see a shadow."

10. "The only person you are destined to become is the person you decide to be."

11. "An eye for an eye only ends up making the whole world blind."

12. "Do not wait for the last autumn, flowers of the spring may never come."

13. "He is a poor player who waits for the dice to be loaded."

14. "Look well to your thoughts, they become your words. Look well to your words, they become your deeds. Look well to your deeds, they become your habits. Look well to your habits, they become your destiny."

15. "There is no remedy for love but to love more."

16. "The more a man has, the more he wants."

17. "The greatest good you can do for someone is not just to share your riches, but to reveal to them their own."

18. "Wrinkles should merely tell a story of where the smiles have been."

19. "Don't wait for extraordinary opportunities. Seize common ones and make them extraordinary."

20. "Opportunity is missed by most people because it comes dressed in overalls and looks like work."

21. "The more I learn, the more I realize how much I don't know."

22. "A man without courage is a man without faith."

23. "The foundation of happiness is not money, but relationship with those we love."

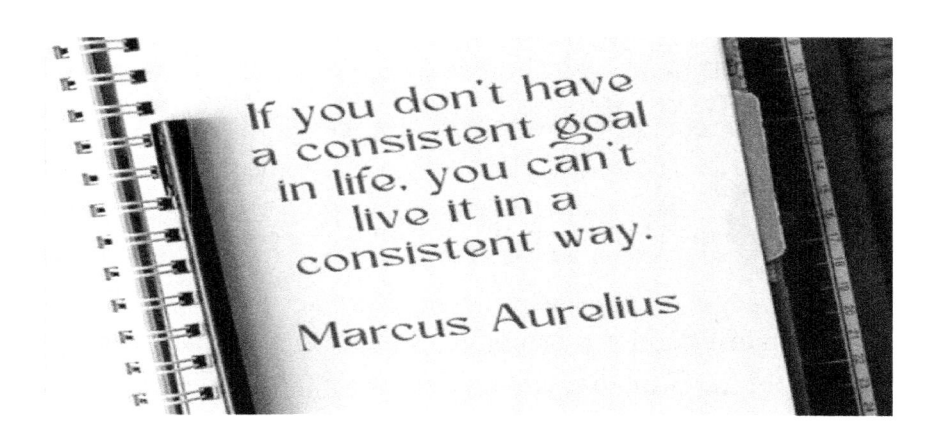

****

> If you don't have a consistent goal in life, you can't live it in a consistent way.
>
> Marcus Aurelius

23. Honore De Balzac

Novelist, Playwright

Nationality: French

Born: May 20, 1799, in Tours, France

Death: August 18, 1850, in Paris, France

Age: 51

Author of "La Comédie Humaine," a series of interlinked novels portraying French society.

1. "Behind every great fortune lies a crime."

2. "All that I am, or hope to be, I owe to my angel mother."

3. "A woman is the future of man."

4. "A man's errors are more instructive than his achievements."

5. "To create something truly great, one must first lose himself in the idea."

6. "The heart of a mother is a deep abyss at the bottom of which you will always find forgiveness."

7. "Hope is a good breakfast, but it is a bad supper."

8. "Money is only a tool; it will not buy happiness, but poverty prevents you from buying anything at all."

9. "Man is a rope, tied at one end to the animal and at the other to the superhuman."

10. "The only way to deal with an unfree world is to become so absolutely free that your very existence is an act of rebellion."

11. "Love conquers all things, even the impossible."

12. "Every misfortune is an opportunity in disguise."

13. "There is no friend like an old friend."

14. "Happiness is a secret between the body and the soul."

15. "Paris is not a city, it is an abyss."

16. "The greatest remedy for those who are afraid, lonely or unhappy is to go outside, somewhere where they can be quite alone with the heavens, nature and God."

17. "Every man over forty is responsible for his face."

18. "Silence is a true friend who never betrays."

19. "The misfortune of the world is that the stupid are so certain of

themselves, while the wise are so full of doubt."

20. "Love is like a game of chess, the player who hesitates is lost."

21. "There is no happiness without gratitude."

22. "A great fire illuminates even the smallest objects."

23. "The tragedy of life is not death, but what we let die within us while we live."

24. "To achieve great things, two things are necessary: a plan and not quite enough time."

25. "A woman's life is a symphony; a man's a novel."

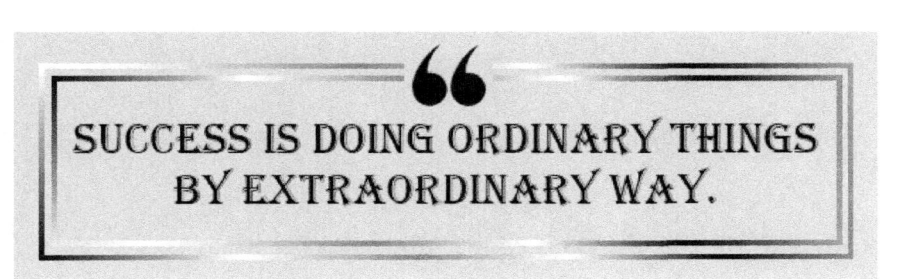

****

> **SUCCESS IS DOING ORDINARY THINGS BY EXTRAORDINARY WAY.**

24. Horace

Roman Poet

Nationality: Roman (Ancient Roman)

Born: December 8, 65 BC,
in Venusia, Roman Republic (now Venosa, Italy)

Death: November 27, 8 BC,
in Rome, Roman Republic (now Italy)

Age: 76 (Approx.)

Celebrated poet of the Augustan Age in Rome, known for his odes and satires.

1. "Mediocrity is the bane of the human intellect."

2. "Carpe diem! Pluck the day, live intensely, and don't let it get away!"

3. "He who hesitates is lost."

4. "Wine warms the blood, poetry the soul."

5. "Anger is a brief madness."

6. "The greatest wealth is contentment with little."

7. "Silence is the true ornament of speech."

8. "Speak, if you have anything to say. If not, keep quiet."

9. "Let us eat, drink, and merry, for tomorrow we die." (While a misinterpretation of Horace's original intent, it remains a common and impactful adage.)

10. "A fool's paradise is paved with good intentions."

11. "Where envy reigns, no virtue dwells."

12. "The more a man has, the more he wants."

13. "The measure of life is not its length, but its use."

14. "Beware of judging a book by its cover."

15. "He who conquers himself is the greatest warrior."

16. "Fortune helps the bold."

17. "Love and hate are twins."

18. "Wine brings out the truth."

19. "All that glitters is not gold."

20. "Opportunity does not knock twice."

21. "He who learns but does not think, is lost. He who thinks but does not

learn, is in great danger."

22. "Wine, women, and song, distract men from thoughts of war."

23. "The truest test of a civilization is in the way it treats its weak and helpless."

24. "A friend in need is a friend indeed."

25. "Seize the day, Live for today, Laugh and rejoice. Let the future go its way, Embrace the present moment."

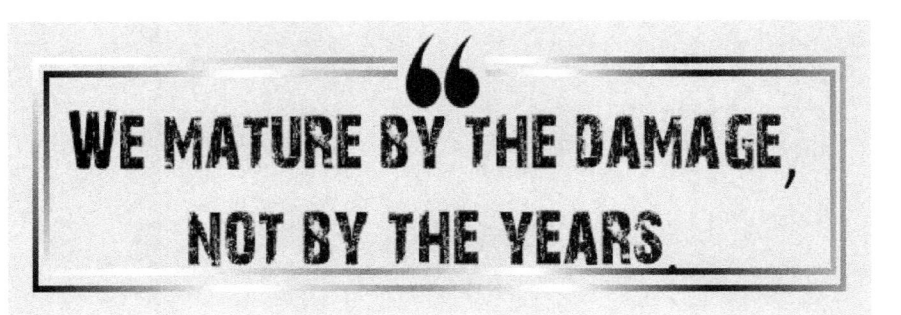

****

> **WE MATURE BY THE DAMAGE, NOT BY THE YEARS**

25. Jean De La Fontaine

Poet, Fabulist

Nationality: French

Born: July 8, 1621, in Château-Thierry, France

Death: April 13, 1695, in Paris, France

Age: 73

Renowned for his fables, such as "The Hare and the Tortoise."

1. "Mediocrity is the bane of the human intellect."

2. "Carpe diem! Pluck the day, live intensely, and don't let it get away!"

3. "He who hesitates is lost."

4. "Wine warms the blood, poetry the soul."

5. "Anger is a brief madness."

6. "The greatest wealth is contentment with little."

7. "Silence is the true ornament of speech."

8. "Speak, if you have anything to say. If not, keep quiet."

9. "Let us eat, drink, and merry, for tomorrow we die." (While a misinterpretation of Horace's original intent, it remains a common and impactful adage.)

10. "A fool's paradise is paved with good intentions."

11. "Where envy reigns, no virtue dwells."

12. "The more a man has, the more he wants."

13. "The measure of life is not its length, but its use."

14. "Beware of judging a book by its cover."

15. "He who conquers himself is the greatest warrior."

16. "Fortune helps the bold."

17. "Love and hate are twins."

18. "Wine brings out the truth."

19. "All that glitters is not gold."

20. "Opportunity does not knock twice."

21. "He who learns but does not think, is lost. He who thinks but does not

learn, is in great danger."

22. "Wine, women, and song, distract men from thoughts of war."

23. "The truest test of a civilization is in the way it treats its weak and helpless."

24. "A friend in need is a friend indeed."

25. "Seize the day, Live for today, Laugh and rejoice. Let the future go its way, Embrace the present moment."

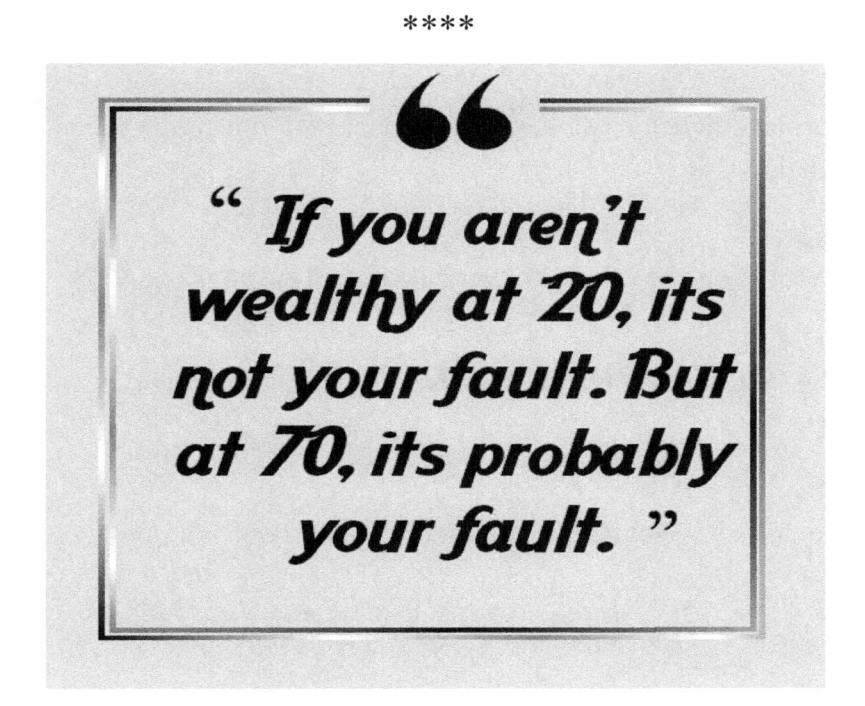

****

> " If you aren't wealthy at 20, its not your fault. But at 70, its probably your fault. "

26. Jim Rohn

Motivational Speaker, Author

Nationality: American

Born: September 17, 1930,
in Yakima, Washington, USA

Death: December 5, 2009,
in Beverly Hills, California, USA

Age: 79

Influential motivational speaker and personal development expert.

1. "Either you run the day, or the day runs you."

2. "Formal education will make you a living; self-education will make you a fortune."

3. "Discipline is the bridge between goals and accomplishments."

4. "The difference between ordinary and extraordinary is that little extra."

5. "Don't wish it was easier, wish you were better."

6. "If you're not moving forward, you're falling behind."

7. "Goals are not reached by luck or by chance, they are reached by hard work and perseverance."

8. "Challenges are what make life interesting and overcoming them is what makes life meaningful."

9. "Learn from the mistakes of others. You can't live long enough to make them all yourself."

10. "Adversity is like a strong wind. It doesn't blow out the candles of those who have no light, but it fans the flames of those who do."

11. "Invest in yourself. It's the best investment you will ever make."

12. "Surround yourself with the best people you can find, they will elevate you."

13. "Don't let yesterday take up too much of today."

14. "Happiness is not something you achieve, it's a way of living."

15. "The more you praise and celebrate your life, the more there is in life to celebrate."

16. "Gratitude unlocks the fullness of life. It turns what we have into enough, and more."

17. "Don't let small minds convince you that your dreams are too big."

18. "The only place where success comes before work is in the dictionary."

19. "Small choices create big changes."

20. "The key to achievement is getting started."

21. "Don't let what you cannot do interfere with what you can do."

22. "Life is an opportunity, benefit from it. Life is a beauty, admire it. Life is a dream, realize it. Life is a challenge, meet it. Life is a duty, complete it."

23. "If you are not willing to risk the usual, you will have to settle for the ordinary."

24. "The best time to plant a tree was 20 years ago. The second best time is now."

****

27. Johann Wolfgang Von Goethe

Poet, Playwright

Nationality: German

Born: August 28, 1749, in Frankfurt, Holy Roman Empire (now Germany)

Death: March 22, 1832, in Weimar, German Confederation (now Germany)

Age: 82

Celebrated for his literary works, including "Faust" and "The Sorrows of Young Werther."

1. "Think big thoughts but relish small pleasures."

2. "He who does not advance every day, falls back."

3. "Knowing yourself is the greatest wisdom."

4. "There are two things which men never fully appreciate – one is time, the other water – and when they are gone, their worth is recognized."

5. "Dwell not on the past, it takes away from the present."

6. "Nothing so strengthens the mind as the ability to bear misfortune."

7. "The only person you are destined to become is the person you decide to be."

8. "A small garden, a library, and a few friends suffice."

9. "Whoever cannot find a quiet corner in his own heart cannot know peace."

10. "Mistakes are like stars in the darkness. You stumble but they show you the way."

11. "Two things alone matter: for one to have what one truly desires, and for one to be content with what one has."

12. "Where the true artist arrives, nature stops and art begins."

13. "Learning in youth is like carving in stone, learning in old age is like carving in water."

14. "He who controls himself controls destiny."

15. "Silence is the most powerful scream."

16. "There are things which cannot be put into words. They remain unspeakable; they can only be experienced."

17. "Doubt kills more dreams than failure ever will."

18. "A small fire easily warms one; a large one devours."

19. "Time is long, but life is short."

20. "Do not wait for the last autumn, flowers of the spring may never come."

21. "The best remedy for those who are afraid, lonely or unhappy is to go outside, somewhere where they can be quite alone with the heavens, nature and God."

22. "Treat people as if they were what they ought to be and you help them to become what they are capable of being."

23. "The happiest people are those who think the most pleasant thoughts."

24. "The more a man has, the more he wants."

25. "A man's errors are more instructive than his achievements."

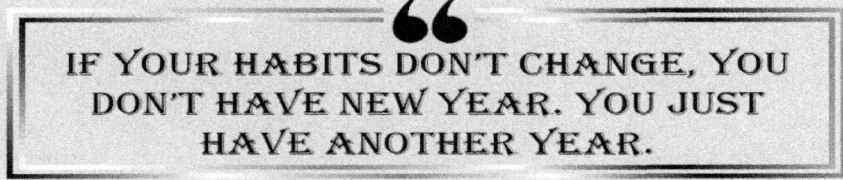

****

> IF YOUR HABITS DON'T CHANGE, YOU DON'T HAVE NEW YEAR. YOU JUST HAVE ANOTHER YEAR.

28. Jonathan Swift

Author, Satirist

Nationality: Irish (born in England)

Born: November 30, 1667, in Dublin, Ireland

Death: October 19, 1745, in Dublin, Ireland

Age: 77 (approx.)

Author of "Gulliver's Travels" and famous for his satirical writings.

1. "May you live all the days of your life."

2. "A man is most uneasy when he is at rest."

3. "Whoever wants a perfect friend in this world will bear its imperfections."

4. "Wisdom is often found in unexpected places."

5. "No man was ever wise by means of mud."

6. "As for your reason - be a little careful of it; it is a delicate instrument when not meddled with."

7. "A satire is a looking-glass, wherein everyone sees everyone but

himself."

8. "Hope is a good breakfast, but it is a bad supper."

9. "It is useless to attempt to reason a man out of a thing he has been reasoned into."

10. "Travel, in the younger sort, is a part of education; in the elder, a part of experience."

11. "Clothes and accomplishments wear well, but both must be changed often."

12. "He that cannot conceal his folly will be forever wise in his own conceit."

13. "He who tells a lie once is not believed when he tells a truth."

14. "Never go to bed angry."

15. "No wise man ever wished to be younger."

16. "Every man's fortune hangs from the uncertainty of a die."

17. "A man with an empty stomach and a head full of ideas is a very dangerous person."

18. "He is happiest who lives forgotten while enjoying quiet pleasures."

19. "Those who would govern the world must first learn to govern themselves."

20. "Never lend money to a friend; it ends the friendship forever."

21. "The only way to deal with an unfree world is to become so absolutely free that your very existence is an act of rebellion."

22. "A great fire illuminates even the smallest objects."

23. "Silence is the true ornament of speech."

24. "The reason why so few people become great is because so few people are willing to be ridiculous."

****

> **Don't care who is doing better than you. Care about what you are doing now Vs last time.**

29. Lucius Annaeus Seneca

Philosopher, Statesman

Nationality: Roman (Ancient Roman)

Born: 4 BC (approximately), in Corduba, Hispania (now Córdoba, Spain)

Death: AD 65, in Rome, Roman Empire

Age: 69 (approx.)

Stoic philosopher and advisor to Emperor Nero.

1. "Life is not simply living, but living well."

2. "A short life and a merry one is better than a long and miserable one."

3. "Happiness is a matter of perspective."

4. "Fortune favors the bold."

5. "While we wait, the time already passes."

6. "Anger and grief are poor advisors."

7. "Waste no time arguing about what a good man should be. Be one."

8. "Never be ashamed to admit you have been wrong. Which is just

another way of saying you are wiser today than yesterday."

9. "True freedom lies in controlling yourself, not external circumstances."

10. "Quality, not quantity, is the measure of life."

11. "Tell me how a man dies, and I will tell you how he lived."

12. "If a thing exists, the possibility of achieving it exists."

13. "Difficulties strengthen the mind, just as labor does the body."

14. "Love the art, not the artist."

15. "The greatest remedy for those who are afraid, lonely or unhappy is to go outside, somewhere where they can be quite alone with the heavens, nature and God."

16. "He who fears death is afraid of everything."

17. "Live today as if it were your last."

18. "Wine warms the blood, poetry the soul."

19. "No man was ever wise by means of mud."

20. "The time is long, but life is short."

21. "Gratitude is not only the greatest virtue, but the parent of all others."

22. "Sow a thought, reap an action; sow an action, reap a habit; sow a habit, reap a character; sow a character, reap a destiny."

23. "There are two things which men never fully appreciate – one is time, the other water – and when they are gone, their worth is recognized."

24. "It is not that we have a short time to live, but that we waste a lot of it."

25. "Don't watch the clock; do what it does. Keep going."

****

> I forgive people.
> It doesn't mean I accept their behavior or trust them again. It means I forgive them for me, so I can let go and move on with my life.

30. Mae West

Actress, Playwright

Nationality: American

Born: August 17, 1893,
in Brooklyn, New York, USA

Death: November 22, 1980,
in Hollywood, California, USA

Age: 87

Iconic actress known for her wit and sensuality in Hollywood's Golden Age.

1. "Goodness is something you do in the dark."

2. "Men are like streetcars. If you miss one, there's always another along."

3. "Marriage is a good thing – but don't let it go to your head."

4. "Be good. If you can't be good, be bad – but magnificent."

5. "Beauty fades, diamonds are forever."

6. "Sex is power, and I intend to use it."

7. "It's not the men in my life that count, it's the life in my men."

8. "Keep a diary and one day it will keep you."

9. "I'm glad I'm a woman – even if I have to pretend to be a lady."

10. "The more a man learns, the less he talks."

11. "My curves are not accidental."

12. "A little sugar makes the medicine go down."

13. "You only live once, but if you do it right, once is enough."

14. "I never said I was good, I just said I was the best."

15. "Why do good girls get better parts? I'm tired of playing good girls."

16. "Come up and see me sometime." (Her iconic line from Diamond Lil)

17. "Age is just a number. It doesn't matter to me how old I am. I can still do the splits."

18. "The reason I wrote my own plays is that I like talking about myself."

19. "If I'm a bad example, then that's just great. It means I've got character."

20. "The hardest thing to keep a secret is your age."

21. "The important thing is to keep the ball rolling."

22. "I never lose. I either win or I learn."

23. "Too much of anything is just enough."

24. "Don't marry a man in haste just because you're late."

25. "Life is short, wear a low-cut dress."

****

> Everyone need something to aim for. You can call it a challenge or you can call it a goal. It is what make us human. It is challenges that take us from being caveman to reach for the stars

31. Marcus Tullius Cicero

Roman Statesman, Orator

Nationality: Roman (Ancient Roman)

Born: January 3, 106 BC, in Arpinum, Roman Republic (now Arpino, Italy)

Death: December 7, 43 BC, in Formia, Roman Republic (now Italy)

Age: 63

Renowned Roman orator, lawyer, and statesman, known for his speeches and philosophical writings.

1. "Friendship doubles our joys and divides our sorrows."

2. "A house is not made with bricks and mortar, but with laughter and love."

3. "Silence is eloquence in its best form."

4. "The greater wealth is contentment with little."

5. "Not to know what has happened before you is to be always a child."

6. "Gratitude is not only the greatest virtue, but the parent of all others."

7. "The worth of a thing is known by the price that it is fetched."

8. "Justice without courage is weak; courage without justice is arrogant."

9. "An eye for an eye only ends up making the whole world blind."

10. "He who laughs without reason is a fool."

11. "The foundation of liberty is justice."

12. "The laws all men have in common derive from reason alone."

13. "The good fortune of friends is our own."

14. "Bad laws are worse than none."

15. "A friend in need is a friend indeed."

16. "The good are always bold; the wicked are always cowardly."

17. "Time heals all wounds."

18. "To live is the rarest thing in the world. Most people exist, that is all."

19. "Education is the foundation of true freedom."

20. "Old age is a shipwreck."

21. "There is no excuse for ignorance in those who have the ability to

learn."

22. "The opposite of courage in disaster is not cowardice, but rashness."

23. "A man's best friend is himself."

24. "He who can conquer himself is the greatest warrior."

25. "Let your sleep be a crown that gently refreshes you for the waking hours."

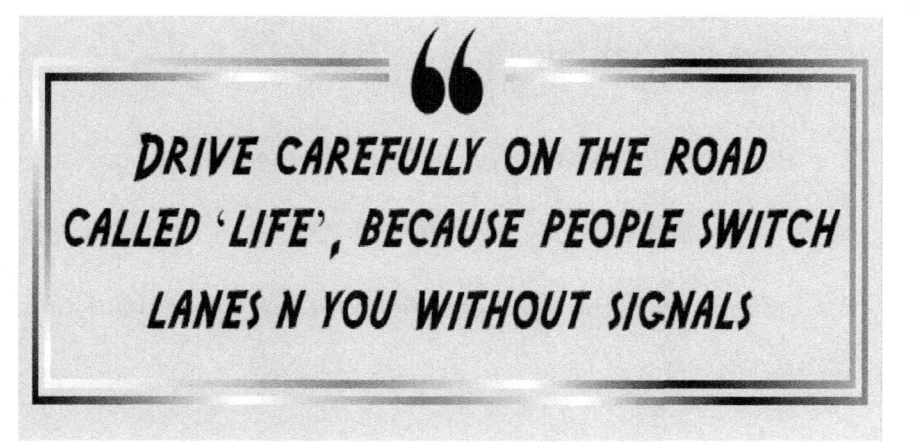

****

> **DRIVE CAREFULLY ON THE ROAD CALLED 'LIFE', BECAUSE PEOPLE SWITCH LANES N YOU WITHOUT SIGNALS**

32. Mark Twain

Author, Humorist

Nationality: American

Born: November 30, 1835, in Florida, Missouri, USA

Death: April 21, 1910, in Redding, Connecticut, USA

Age: 74

Famous for "The Adventures of Tom Sawyer" and "Adventures of Huckleberry Finn."

1. "The secret of getting ahead is getting started."

2. "Never argue with stupid people, they'll drag you down to their level and beat you with experience."

3. "The two most important days in your life are the day you are born and the day you find out why."

4. "It's not the size of the dog in the fight, it's the size of the fight in the dog."

5. "Don't let schooling interfere with your education."

6. "Clothes make the man. Naked people have little or no influence on society."

7. "Get your facts first, then you can distort them as much as you please."

8. "Age is an issue of mind over matter. If you don't mind, it doesn't matter."

9. "Comparison is the death of joy."

10. "There are lies, damned lies, and statistics."

11. "I have never met a man so stupid that he couldn't teach me something."

12. "The difference between the right word and the almost right word is the difference between lightning and a lightning bug."

13. "The only way to be a good sport is to lose all the time."

14. "The best time to plant a tree was 20 years ago. The second best time is now."

15. "Everybody complains about the weather, but nobody does anything about it."

16. "An honest politician is one who stays bought."

17. "Whiskey is for drinking, water is for fighting over."

18. "A man who carries a cat by the tail learns something he can't learn by sitting on a cushion."

19. "There is no such thing as bad weather, only bad clothes."

20. "Go to heaven for the climate, hell for the company."

21. "A lie doesn't have to be a big thing to create a great deal of trouble."

22. "I'm an old man and have many regrets, but not a single one is for taking too many risks."

23. "It's easier to fool people than to convince them they've been fooled."

24. "The more I learn about people, the more I love my dog."

25. "If you tell the truth, you don't have to remember anything."

26. "I am an old man and have many regrets, but not a single one is for taking too many risks."

27. "Humor is the great thing, the saving thing. The more laughter in the world, the better off we are."

28. "The human race has just one really effective weapon - laughter."

29. "Training is everything. The peach was once a bitter almond, cauliflower is nothing but cabbage with college education."

30. "A man in debt is a slave. He is not his own man. The loan shark controls him."

31. "Kindness is a language the deaf can hear and the blind can see."

32. "The only person who is educated is the one who has learned how to learn and change."

33. "Two things are infinite: the universe and human stupidity. And I'm not sure about the universe."

34. "Education is an admirable thing, but it is well to remember that nothing that is taught outside a library is of much account."

35. "Work consists of whatever a body is obliged to do. Play consists of whatever a body is not obliged to do."

36. "The truth is seldom pure and never simple."

37. "He who learns but does not think, is lost. He who thinks but does not learn, is in great danger."

38. "The noblest prospect which a civilized community can present is a library containing within its walls the distilled souls of the living and dead."

39. "There are three kinds of lies: lies, damned lies, and statistics."

40. "The man who does not read good books has no advantage over the man who cannot read them."

41. "Adventure is worthwhile in itself."

42. "It is not what we eat but what we digest that makes us strong."

43. "Patriotism is supporting your country all the time, and your government when it deserves it."

44. "The more I learn about people, the more I love my dog." (Yes, it's so good it bears repetition!)

45. "Never put off till tomorrow what you can do the day after tomorrow."

****

FORGET the Mistake REMEMBER the Lesson

33. Mason Cooley

Aphorist, Academic

Nationality: American

Born: July 1927,
near Cape Cod, Massachusetts, USA

Death: July 25, 2002,
in New York City, New York, USA

Age: 75

Noted for his concise and witty aphorisms on various subjects.

1. "The cure for boredom is curiosity. There is no cure for curiosity."

2. "Reading gives us someplace to go when we have to stay where we are."

3. "A friend accepts us as we are yet helps us to be what we should."

4. "The time I kill is killing me."

5. "Loneliness is never more cruel than when it is felt in close propinquity with someone who has ceased to communicate."

6. "Ideals are an imaginative understanding of that which is desirable in that which is possible."

7. "The folly of endless consumerism sends us on a wild goose-chase for happiness through materialism."

8. "We require a great many comforts to make us comfortable."

9. "We should realize that they are our best selves because they cannot be anything else."

10. "Reading is a discount ticket to everywhere."

11. "The bureaucracy is expanding to meet the needs of the expanding bureaucracy."

12. "Tradition is a guide and not a jailer."

13. "The best time to give advice to your children is while they're still young enough to believe you know what you're talking about."

14. "We have to live with our loneliness and the destiny that shapes it."

15. "The chief product of an automated society is a widespread and deepening sense of boredom."

16. "Some desire is necessary to keep life in motion, and he whose real wants are supplied must admit those of fancy."

17. "One does not devote oneself to art — one is caught up in art."

18. "Anxiety is the poison of human life; the parent of many sins and of more miseries."

19. "The arts and humanities nourish the soul, whereas science and technology feed the body and the mind."

20. "It's especially hard to admit that you made a mistake to someone you care about, but love is about being truthful and sometimes truth hurts."

21. "The greatest gift is the ability to forget — to forget the bad things and focus on the good."

22. "Home is a name, a word, it is a strong one; stronger than a magician ever spoke, or spirit ever answered to, in the strongest conjuration."

23. "Criticism is prejudice made plausible."

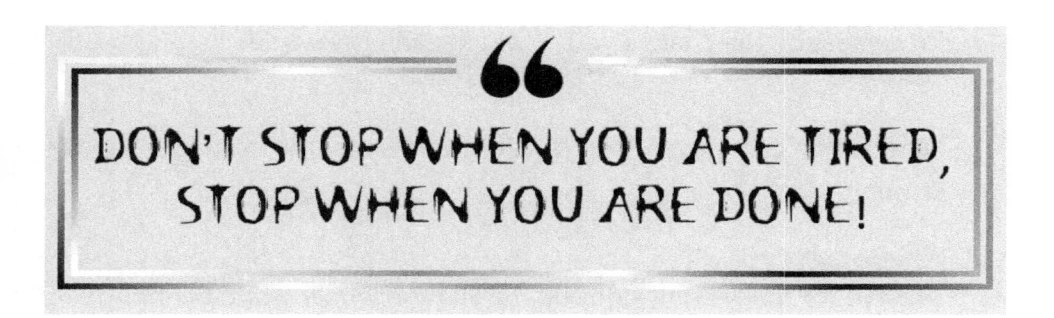

****

" DON'T STOP WHEN YOU ARE TIRED, STOP WHEN YOU ARE DONE!

34. Mohandas (Mahatma) Gandhi

Leader of Indian Independence Movement

Nationality: Indian

Born: October 2, 1869, in Porbandar, British India (now in Gujarat, India)

Death: January 30, 1948, in New Delhi, India

Age: 78

Led India to independence from British rule through nonviolent civil disobedience.

1. "Be the change that you wish to see in the world."

2. "The best way to find yourself is to lose yourself in the service of others."

3. "Live as if you were to die tomorrow. Learn as if you were to live forever."

4. "You must be the change you want to see in the world."

5. "The weak can never forgive. Forgiveness is the attribute of the strong."

6. "An eye for an eye only ends up making the whole world blind."

7. "The future depends on what you do today."

8. "First, they ignore you, then they laugh at you, then they fight you, then you win."

9. "The greatness of a nation and its moral progress can be judged by the way its animals are treated."

10. "Happiness is when what you think, what you say, and what you do are in harmony."

11. "Strength does not come from the body. It comes from the will."

12. "You may never know what results come of your actions, but if you do nothing, there will be no results."

13. "The best way to find yourself is to lose yourself in service to others."

14. "Freedom is not worth having if it does not include the freedom to make mistakes."

15. "The moment there is suspicion about a person's motives, everything he does becomes tainted."

16. "A man is but the product of his thoughts; what he thinks, he becomes."

17. "There is more to life than increasing its speed."

18. "You can chain me, you can torture me, you can even destroy this body, but you will never imprison my mind."

19. "To believe in something, and not to live it, is dishonest."

20. "A small body of determined spirits fired by an unquenchable faith in their mission can alter the course of history."

21. "There is a sufficiency in the world for man's need but not for man's greed."

22. "I will not let anyone walk through my mind with their dirty feet."

23. "My life is my message."

24. "In a gentle way, you can shake the world."

25. "Even if you are a minority of one, the truth is the truth."

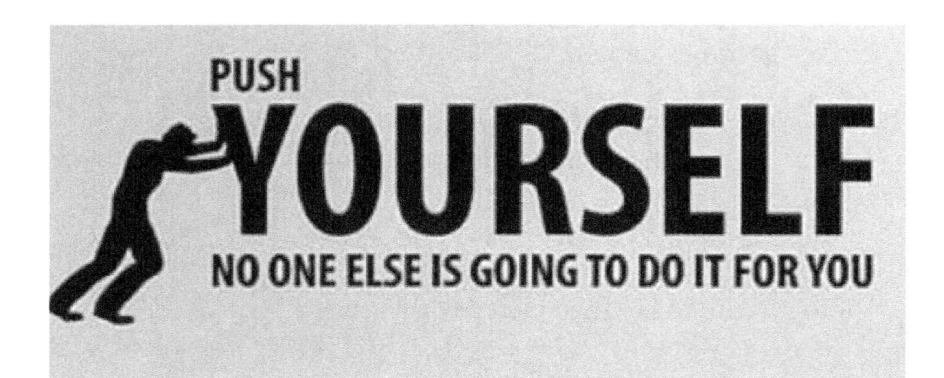

* * * *

PUSH YOURSELF
NO ONE ELSE IS GOING TO DO IT FOR YOU

35. Mother Teresa

Missionary, Humanitarian

Nationality: Albanian (naturalized Indian)

Born: August 26, 1910, in Skopje, Ottoman Empire (now North Macedonia)

Death: September 5, 1997, in Calcutta, India (now Kolkata, India)

Age: 87

Renowned for her work with the poor and marginalized, awarded the Nobel Peace Prize in 1979.

1. "Spread love everywhere you go. Let no one ever come to you without leaving happier."

2. "Kind words can be short and easy to speak, but their echoes are truly endless."

3. "If you judge people, you have no time to love them."

4. "Do not wait for leaders; do it alone, person to person."

5. "Peace begins with a smile."

6. "Not all of us can do great things. But we can do small things with great love."

7. "We cannot all do great things, but we can do small things with great love."

8. "Loneliness and the feeling of being unwanted is the most terrible poverty."

9. "Joy is a net of love by which you can catch souls."

10. "The greatest science in the world, in heaven and on earth, is love."

11. "Let us always meet each other with a smile, for the smile is the beginning of love."

12. "It's not how much we give but how much love we put into giving."

13. "I can do things you cannot, you can do things I cannot; together we can do great things."

14. "Love is not patronizing and charity isn't about pity, it is about love. Charity and love are the same—with charity you give love, so don't just give money but reach out your hand instead."

15. "The hunger for love is much more difficult to remove than the hunger for bread."

16. "Yesterday is gone. Tomorrow has not yet come. We have only today. Let us begin."

17. "If you want a love message to be heard, it has got to be sent out. To keep a lamp burning, we have to keep putting oil in it."

18. "Be faithful in small things because it is in them that your strength lies."

19. "We fear the future because we are wasting the today."

20. "We can do no great things, only small things with great love."

21. "Love to be real, it must cost—it must hurt—it must empty us of self."

22. "God doesn't require us to succeed; he only requires that you try."

23. "We think sometimes that poverty is only being hungry, naked, and homeless. The poverty of being unwanted, unloved, and uncared for is the greatest poverty."

****

36. Napoleon Bonaparte

Military Leader, Emperor

Nationality: French

Born: August 15, 1769, in Ajaccio, Corsica, France

Death: May 5, 1821, in Saint Helena, British Empire

Age: 51

Rose to power as Emperor of the French, known for his military campaigns and the Napoleonic Code.

1. "Victory belongs to the most persevering."

2. "Never interrupt your enemy when he is making a mistake."

3. "A leader is a dealer in hope."

4. "There are moments in life when everything depends on a single minute, on a single action."

5. "The best way to predict the future is to create it."

6. "The greatest danger for most of us is not that our aim is too high and we miss it, but that it is too low and we reach it."

7. "A throne is only a wooden bench covered with velvet."

8. "In war, fortune smiles upon the bold."

9. "Impossible is a word to be found only in the dictionary of fools."

10. "A picture is worth a thousand words."

11. "Leaders who fear to be blamed cannot be praised."

12. "I would rather rule over minds than bodies."

13. "Attack the enemy where he least expects it."

14. "There are but two powers in the world, the sword and the mind. In the long run, the sword is always beaten by the mind."

15. "History is the fiction agreed upon."

16. "A soldier fights not because he hates what is in front of him, but because he loves what is behind him."

17. "The fate of a battle turns on a moment."

18. "Courage is not the absence of fear, but the triumph over it."

19. "Love is a madness, but it is the only one which is ever really sane."

20. "In politics, absurdity is not a handicap."

21. "He who cannot think will perish."

22. "Fear kills more people than the sword."

23. "There is only one vice: ignorance."

24. "I am a lion when it comes to work; a fox when it comes to men."

25. "Education is the passport to the future, for tomorrow belongs to those who believe in the beauty of their dreams."

26. "To live is the rarest thing in the world. Most people exist, that is all."

27. "Silence is the true ornament of speech."

28. "Courage is not the absence of fear, but the triumph over it."

29. "Difficulties increase the nearer we approach the goal."

30. "He who loves the good more than himself loves God."

31. "The time is long, but life is short."

32. "Everyone wants to understand art. Why don't they try to understand the song of a bird?"

33. "It is all about finding new forms."

34. "Do not let schooling interfere with your education."

35. "Beauty fades, diamonds are forever."

36. "There are two things that children should learn - to obey good principles and to despise bad ones."

37. "The death of one man is a small thing, but the extinction of a whole people is an awful calamity."

38. "Be kind, for everyone you meet is fighting a battle you know nothing about."

39. "The only person you are destined to become is the person you decide to be."

40. "There are moments in life when everything depends on a single minute, on a single action."

41. "Imagination rules the world."

****

37. Oscar Wilde

Playwright, Writer

Nationality: Irish

Born: October 16, 1854, in Dublin, Ireland

Death: November 30, 1900, in Paris, France

Age: 46

Celebrated playwright and author known for works like "The Picture of Dorian Gray."

1. "To be good is to be in harmony with one's self."

2. "The truth is rarely pure and never simple."

3. "The only difference between the saint and the sinner is that the saint has a past, and the sinner has a future."

4. "The cynic is the man who knows the price of everything, and the value of nothing."

5. "The reason why a man believes a thing is because he wants to believe it."

6. "Everything in moderation, including moderation."

7. "The only way to get rid of temptation is to yield to it."

8. "Beauty is a form of genius - indeed, the highest form of genius that I know of."

9. "To live is the rarest thing in the world. Most people exist, that is all."

10. "We are all in the gutter, but some of us are looking at the stars."

11. "Education is an admirable thing, but it is well to remember that nothing that is taught outside a library is of much account."

12. "There is no sin except vulgarity."

13. "Be yourself. Everyone else is already taken."

14. "A man cannot be comfortable without his own approval."

15. "The only person who is educated is the one who has learned how to learn and change."

16. "Work is the curse of the drinking classes."

17. "Imitation is the sincerest form of flattery."

18. "The truth is seldom pure and never simple."

19. "A gentleman is one who never remembers a woman's face after he has met her."

20. "The well-bred Englishman abroad is just the English working-class at home."

21. "The undiscoverable is that towards which all knowledge travels."

22. "The only thing to do with good advice is to pass it on. It is never of any use to oneself."

23. "There is no such thing as a good influence - all influence is immoral - immoral or moral it makes no difference."

24. "The future belongs to those who believe in the beauty of their dreams."

25. "To love oneself is the beginning of a lifelong romance."

****

38. Ovid

Poet, Author

Nationality: Roman (Ancient Roman)

Born: March 20, 43 BC, in Sulmo, Roman Republic (now Sulmona, Italy)

Death: AD 17/18, in Tomis, Roman Empire (now Constanța, Romania)

Age: 61 (Approx.)

Renowned for his mythological poetry, including "Metamorphoses."

1. "Seize the day, live for today, laugh and rejoice. Let the future go its way, embrace the present moment."

2. "Wine warms the blood, poetry the soul."

3. "Silence is the true ornament of speech."

4. "The greatest wealth is contentment with little."

5. "There is no remedy for love but to love more." ("Remedium amoris est amor.")

6. "Hope is a good breakfast, but it is a bad supper."

7. "Beauty fades, diamonds are forever."

8. "The time is long, but life is short."

9. "He who hesitates is lost."

10. "Speak, if you have anything to say. If not, keep quiet."

11. "Wine brings out the truth."

12. "All that glitters is not gold."

13. "Opportunity does not knock twice."

14. "The measure of life is not its length, but its use."

15. "Love is a madness, but it is the only one which is ever really sane."

16. "Jealousy is a cruel mistress, she destroys herself while tormenting others."

17. "The gods themselves cannot alter the past."

18. "Ignorance is a curse, for she knows not her own shame."

19. "There is more in a look than in a word."

20. "The more a man has, the more he wants."

21. "He who conquers himself is the greatest warrior."

22. "A small fire easily warms one; a large one devours."

23. "Do not let what you cannot do interfere with what you can do."

24. "The greatest remedy for those who are afraid, lonely or unhappy is to go outside, somewhere where they can be quite alone with the heavens, nature and God."

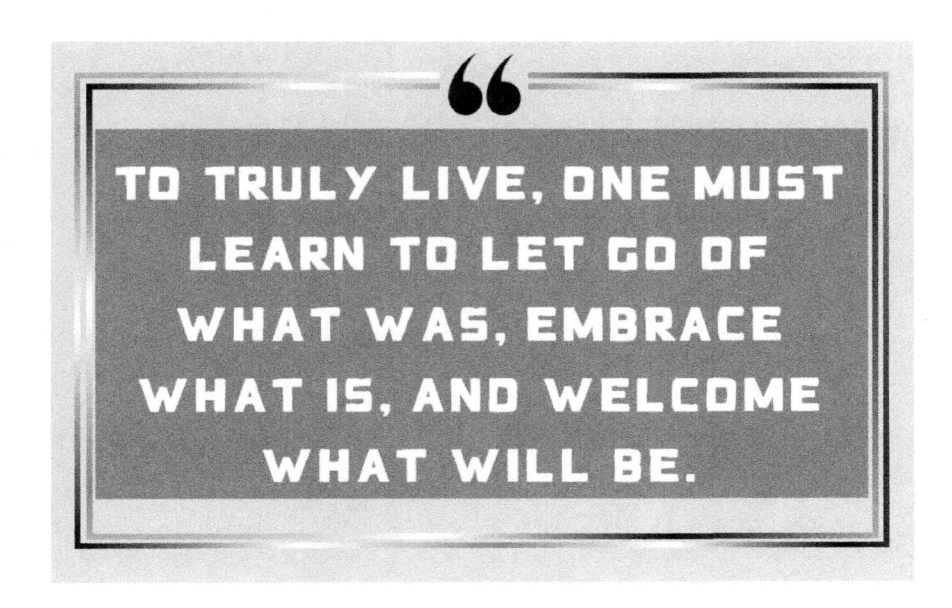

****

> TO TRULY LIVE, ONE MUST LEARN TO LET GO OF WHAT WAS, EMBRACE WHAT IS, AND WELCOME WHAT WILL BE.

39. Pablo Picasso

Painter, Sculptor

Nationality: Spanish (later French)

Born: October 25, 1881, in Málaga, Spain

Death: April 8, 1973, in Mougins, France

Age: 91

Pioneer of modern art, co-founder of Cubism, and creator of iconic works like "Guernica."

1. "Art washes away from the soul the dust of everyday life."

2. "A mistake is an opportunity to make something new."

3. "Learn the rules like a pro, so you can break them like an artist."

4. "Youth is when everything is possible. Age is when everything is still possible."

5. "I paint objects as I think them, not as I see them."

6. "Sculpture is the art of the hole and the lump."

7. "Great artists steal."

8. "Everyone wants to understand art. Why don't they try to understand the song of a bird?"

9. "Computers are useful to solve equations, but not very creative."

10. "Good taste is the enemy of creativity."

11. "Fear kills creativity. Risk brings rewards."

12. "I am always doing that which I cannot do, in order that I may learn how to do it."

13. "Everything you can imagine is real."

14. "It is all about finding new forms."

15. "Don't think so much, feel."

16. "The only rule is there are no rules."

17. "Painters who use words are not painters."

18. "To draw you must close your eyes, and sing."

19. "I always try to do what I don't know how to do."

20. "I make the object. Then I find the name."

21. "Every child is an artist. The problem is how to remain an artist once we grow up."

22. "Mirrors, they reflect what you already have. Art, it shows you what it is possible to have."

****

40. Plato

Philosopher, Teacher

Nationality: Ancient Greek

Born: 427/428 BC, in Athens, Ancient Greece

Death: 347/348 BC, in Athens, Ancient Greece

Age: 80 (Approx.)

Founder of the Academy in Athens, influential in Western philosophy.

1. "The unexamined life is not worth living."

2. "True knowledge is to know the extent of one's ignorance."

3. "Necessity is the mother of invention."

4. "Be kind, for everyone you meet is fighting a battle you know nothing about."

5. "The only true wisdom is in knowing you know nothing."

6. "Music gives a soul to the universe, wings to the mind, flight to the imagination, and life to everything."

7. "Courage is the beginning of wisdom."

8. "Do not let schooling interfere with your education."

9. "Our eyes cannot always see our mistakes, but others can make out ours more easily than their own."

10. "Philosophy begins in wonder."

11. "There are two things that children should learn - to obey good principles and to despise bad ones."

12. "The death of one man is a small thing, but the extinction of a whole people is an awful calamity."

13. "A lie told once might be overlooked, but a lie repeated is unpardonable."

14. "Be silent or speak words that are worth the silence."

15. "Love can cause pain, but refusing to love will cause more."

16. "He who learns but does not think, is lost. He who thinks but does not learn, is in great danger."

17. "Time is the greatest innovator."

18. "The worst form of injustice is to try to make unequal things equal."

19. "The measure of a man is the way he handles the unexpected."

20. "Wise men talk because they have something to say; fools talk because they have to say something."

21. "The greatest remedy for those who are afraid, lonely or unhappy is to go outside, somewhere where they can be quite alone with the heavens, nature and God."

22. "You can easily tell the quality of a society by its music."

23. "There are good people in every profession, except the barbers – they have to deal with so many knaves."

24. "Democracy is the worst form of government except for all those other forms that have been tried from time to time."

****

> **IF NOBODY HATES YOU, YOU ARE DOING SOMETHING WRONG.**

41. Ralph Waldo Emerson

Philosopher, Essayist

Nationality: American

Born: May 25, 1803, in Boston, Massachusetts, USA

Death: April 27, 1882, in Concord, Massachusetts, USA

Age: 78

Leading figure in the transcendentalist movement and author of essays like "Self-Reliance."

1. "Do not go where the path may lead, go instead where there is no path and leave a trail."

2. "What lies behind us and what lies before us are tiny matters compared to what lies within us."

3. "The only person you are destined to become is the person you decide to be."

4. "It is not the length of a life, but the depth of it."

5. "Do not follow where the path may lead. Go instead where there is no path and leave a trail."

6. "Whoso would be a man must be a nonconformist."

7. "Nothing great is ever achieved without enthusiasm."

8. "Shallow men believe in luck. Strong men believe in cause and effect."

9. "The greatest glory in living lies not in never falling, but in rising every time we fall."

10. "Trust thyself, every heart vibrates to that iron string."

11. "A foolish consistency is the hobgoblin of little minds."

12. "The earth laughs in flowers."

13. "To be yourself in a world that is constantly trying to make you something else is the greatest accomplishment."

14. "Beauty is not caused. It is."

15. "To write a line that is simple and true is a great thing."

16. "Friendship is the inexpressible comfort of feeling safe with a person, having neither to weigh your thoughts nor measure your words."

17. "The years teach much which the days never knew."

18. "Doubt is not a pleasant condition, but certainty is absurd."

19. "A good laugh over any good story is worth a hundred sermons."

20. "Do not importune nature for gifts of healing; work with her and obtain health."

21. "To win without risk is to triumph without glory."

22. "Society needs every pair of helping hands."

23. "The ornament of a house is the friends who frequent it."

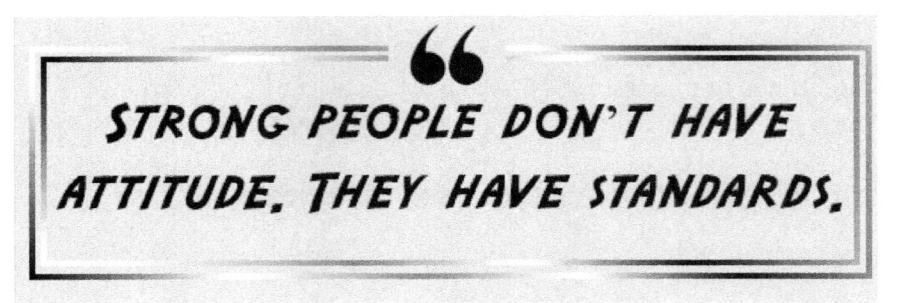

****

> **STRONG PEOPLE DON'T HAVE ATTITUDE. THEY HAVE STANDARDS.**

42. Robert Frost

Poet

Nationality: American

Born: March 26, 1874, in San Francisco, California, USA

Death: January 29, 1963, in Boston, Massachusetts, USA

Age: 88

Four-time Pulitzer Prize-winning poet known for his rural and nature-themed poetry.

1. "Two roads diverged in a yellow wood, And sorry I could not travel both And be one traveler, long I stood And looked down one as far as I could..."

2. "The woods are lovely, dark and deep, But I have promises to keep, And miles to go before I sleep, And miles to go before I sleep."

3. "Nature is not what you see - Nature is what we feel."

4. "I learned more about the Earth by losing my apple than by finding Newton's."

5. "Men are caught not in a material trap, but in a net of nervous reactions."

6. "I hold your hand in mine, As if in mine, the hand of fate."

7. "The best way to way to outdo any day is to love the next one more than this one."

8. "Education is the ability to listen to almost anything without losing your temper or your good manners."

9. "Forgive, O Lord, my little jokes, My small self-righteous criteria, And if at last my earthy plot I must resign, O keep its grass from growing wild at will, Give it some chance to do my bidding still."

10. "The figure a poem makes is a poem."

11. "Don't think you have to write when you're not in the mood."

12. "The fact is the sweetest dream that labor knows."

13. "Poetry is a deals in parts of speech of what a bell does in sound."

14. "The earth may be ours but not to have our way with."

15. "I'm never scared when I'm alone."

16. "No tears in the writer, no tears in the reader."

17. "What I hear on the wind is the murmur of a people dissatisfied."

18. "The brain is as wide as the sky."

19. "Poetry is when an emotion has found its thought and the thought has found words."

20. "The only sure thing about going somewhere is that you don't go home."

21. "The poet is the priest of beauty because the priest celebrates what he sees, and the poet makes what he sees."

22. "I'm not a teacher, but an awakener."

23. "The greatest thing that can happen to any child is to discover that he is an artist."

24. "In three words I can sum up everything I've learned about life: it goes on."

25. "To make a poem, take a lump of reality and put it in the imagination's oven; bake it well, then take it out and eat it."

****

> **CONSISTENCY**
> IS WHAT TRANSFORMS AVERAGE
> INTO EXCELLENCE

43. Samuel Butler

Author, Satirist

Nationality: British (English)
Born: December 4, 1835, in Langar, England
Death: June 18, 1902, in London, England

Age: 66

Notable for his satirical novel "Erewhon" and essays.

1. "Every saint has a past, and every sinner a future."

2. "What the superior man thinks is not easily said. What the inferior man thinks is easily said."

3. "The only way to make the best of it is to make the most of it."

4. "All is flux, nothing stays still."

5. "Doubt is not a pleasant condition, but certainty is absurd."

6. "The love of money is the root of all evil." (paraphrasing 1 Timothy 6:10)

7. "Any philosophy which starts by saying 'if' is probably barking up the wrong tree."

8. "The difference between the foolish and the wise is that the foolish man glories in what he knows, while the wise man glories in what he can learn."

9. "All great truths are akin to great secrets; for to say them clearly is to explain away their mystery."

10. "Art is nature, but seen through a temperament."

11. "What is the use of a book without pictures or conversations?" (referencing Lewis Carroll's Alice's Adventures in Wonderland)

12. "Happiness is a butterfly; the more you chase it, the more it eludes you, but if you stand still, it may alight upon you."

13. "The greatest crime which a man can commit against himself is to let himself go to seed."

14. "The older I grow, the more I am convinced that the wisest course in life is to spend your time reading the best books. There are, of course, some very good people, but there are not as many as there are good books."

15. "It is better to have loved and lost than never to have loved at all." (paraphrasing Tennyson's In Memoriam A.H.H.)

16. "The only thing constant in life is change."

17. "The difference between a wise man and a fool is that a wise man learns from his mistakes, and a fool repeats them."

18. "The greatest compliment that was ever paid to me was when I was called a crank. It is an immense compliment to be taken for a man who dares to think for himself."

19. "The only real mistake is the one from which we learn nothing."

20. "The greatest friend of truth is Time, her greatest enemy Prejudice, and her constant companion Humility."

21. "The only person who is educated is the one who has learned how to learn and change."

22. "The only way to get rid of temptation is to yield to it. Resist it, and your soul grows sick with longing for the things it has forbidden to itself."

23. "The greatest tragedy in life is not death, but living a life without purpose."

24. "The only person who is completely satisfied with life is the one who is dead."

*****

44. Samuel Johnson

Lexicographer, Essayist

Nationality: English (British)

Born: September 18, 1709, in Lichfield, England

Death: December 13, 1784, in London, England

Age: 75

Created "A Dictionary of the English Language" and a leading literary figure of the 18th century.

1. "Patriotism is the last refuge of a scoundrel."

2. "Knowledge is not enough. We must apply it. Will is not enough. We must do it."

3. "Whoever has made a good thing better has done well."

4. "A man should keep his friendship in constant repair."

5. "Depend upon it, sir, when a man knows he is wrong, he should readily acknowledge his error."

6. "Clear your mind of cant."

7. "The use of traveling is to regulate imagination with reality, and instead of thinking how things may be, to see them as they are."

8. "He who makes a beast of himself gets rid of the trouble of thinking."

9. "The biographical work is, perhaps, the best kind of history... the life of a great man, minutely examined, will let us into more knowledge of the times than the most voluminous annals."

10. "No private man has too little, if he is satisfied."

11. "Children, like vegetables, thrive best in the open air."

12. "When a man is tired of London, he is tired of life; for there is in London all that life can afford."

13. "Great works are performed not by strength, but by perseverance."

14. "Keep company with people better than yourself; for better will do you good, but equal will never improve you."

15. "He that is learned only at second hand is like a man who lights his candle at another's torch."

16. "No man but a blockhead ever wrote except for money."

17. "Talkers are no good doers."

18. "The true measure of a man is how he treats someone who can do him no good."

19. "Claret for boys, port for men, brandy for heroes."

20. "The way to learn any language is to begin to speak it."

21. "A book that is well written comes over fresh the second time and turns out to be actually better."

22. "Nothing will ever be attempted if only difficulties are considered."

23. "Every man has a right to be his own judge in everything that only respects himself."

24. "Whoever writes a book thinks himself wiser than the whole world."

****

> I forgive people. It doesn't mean I accept their behavior or trust them again. It means I forgive them for me, so I can let go and move on with my life.

45. Sophocles

Playwright, Dramatist

Nationality: Ancient Greek

Born: 497/6 BC,
in Colonus, Ancient Athens, Greece

Death: 406/5 BC, in Athens, Ancient Greece

Age: 90 (Approx.)

Renowned Greek playwright, known for tragedies like "Oedipus Rex."

1. "No man is a failure who has a friend."

2. "The only true wisdom is in knowing you know nothing."

3. "Silence is a true friend who never betrays."

4. "Hope is a good breakfast, but it is a bad supper."

5. "One word frees us of all the weight and pain of life: That word is love."

6. "Small things make up the great."

7. "Excess of anything always turns against itself and brings forth unforeseen and unwanted results."

8. "What is hidden will be told, and what is covered will be revealed."

9. "Man's greatest strength is also his greatest weakness."

10. "The gods envy those who prosper too much."

11. "The course of history may proceed by chance, but the individual's will is master of his own fate."

12. "Justice, when she overtakes us, comes with crushing force."

13. "A single lie destroys a hundred truths."

14. "He who learns must suffer. And even in suffering, learning will bring pain."

15. "We must be willing to let go of the life we planned in order to have the life that is waiting for us."

16. "Speak, that I may see thee."

17. "He who knows himself, knows God."

18. "The man who asks a question is a fool for a minute, the man who does not ask is a fool for life."

19. "The only thing worse than being blind is having sight but no vision."

20. "Happiness is a butterfly; the more you chase it, the more it eludes you, but if you stand still, it may alight upon you."

21. "The time is always ripe to do right."

22. "The truth will set you free, but first it will piss you off."

23. "A small error may lead to a great catastrophe."

24. "Fate hangs precariously in the balance, ever shifting, now this way, now that."

****

> Talent is cheaper than the table salt. What separates the talented individual one is a lot of hard word.

46. Steven Wright

Comedian, Actor

Nationality: American

Born: December 6, 1955, in Cambridge, Massachusetts, USA

Death: -

Age: -

Stand-up comedian known for his deadpan humor and one-liners.

1. "I was born with a glass eye. My parents didn't want me to feel left out, so they bought me a glass leg."

2. "I used to be indecisive, but now I'm not so sure."

3. "If you're not part of the solution, you're part of the precipitate."

4. "I went to the bank and asked the teller for change. She asked me, 'What kind?' I said, 'Anything. Some nickels, dimes, pennies – something I can jingle in my pocket when I walk.' She gave me a brochure for a savings account."

5. "I got a free sample of shampoo in the mail the other day. It's supposed to give you thicker hair, but I'm not sure how I can tell. I haven't had any hair for the past 20 years."

6. "I bought some shoes from a drug dealer. I don't know what he laced

them with, but I've been tripping all day."

7. "I took the SAT's. I got 400 on the math section. They told me I wasn't ready for college. I said, 'I wasn't ready for high school either!'"

8. "I went to a seafood disco last night. Lots of shellfish dancing."

9. "I used to have a fear of public speaking. Now I have a fear of not having a fear of public speaking."

10. "I bought some antidepressants from a drug dealer. He said, 'Take these with milk.' I said, 'But I don't have any milk.' He said, 'Go buy some. Milk is good for your bones.' I said, 'But I don't have any bones.' He said, 'Go buy some.'"

11. "I used to work in a shoe store. Someone came in and asked for loafers. I said, 'Do you have a warrant?'"

12. "I'm on a seafood diet. I see food, and I eat it."

13. "I went to the zoo the other day. It was pretty empty. The only animal there was a dog. It was a shih tzu. I kept asking the zookeeper why it was there. He said, 'We're having a shih tzu exhibition.' I said, 'Is that an all-day thing?'"

14. "I like to do dangerous things. Like eating alphabet soup one letter at a time."

15. "I took a taxi to the library the other day. The driver asked me if I wanted to go around the block. I said, 'No, I'm just returning this book.'"

16. "I met a guy who was addicted to soap. He was clean, but he couldn't stop lathering."

17. "I went to the doctor and told him I broke my arm in two places. He told me to stop going to those places."

18. "I used to be addicted to caffeine. Then I quit cold turkey. Now I get my kicks from lukewarm Pepsi."

19. "I went to a funeral the other day. It was pretty depressing. They didn't even have any cake."

20. "I'm not sure what's wrong with my brain. I keep thinking I'm a fire engine."

21. "I used to have a fear of heights. Then I fell off a cliff. I'm cured now."

22. "Fate hangs precariously in the balance, ever shifting, now this way, now that."

****

47. Swami Vivekanand

Hindu Monk, Philosopher

Nationality: Indian

Born: January 12, 1863, in Calcutta, India (now Kolkata, India)

Death: July 4, 1902, in, Belur Math, West Bengal, India

Age: 39

Introduced Indian philosophy of Vedanta to the Western world and played a significant role in the spread of Hinduism and yoga in the West.

1. Arise, awake, and stop not until the goal is achieved.

2. In a conflict between the heart and the brain, follow your heart.

3. You cannot believe in God until you believe in yourself.

4. All the powers in the universe are already ours. It is we who have put our hands before our eyes and cry that it is dark.

5. The greatest religion is to be true to your own nature. Have faith in yourselves.

6. Stand up, be bold, and take the blame on your own shoulders. Do not go about throwing mud at other; for all the faults you suffer from, you are the sole and only cause.

7. The moment I have realized God sitting in the temple of every human body, the moment I stand in reverence before every human being and see God in him - that moment I am free from bondage, everything that binds vanishes, and I am free.

8. Each work has to pass through these stages: ridicule, opposition, and then acceptance. Those who think ahead of their time are sure to be misunderstood.

9. The world is the great gymnasium where we come to make ourselves strong.

10. You have to grow from the inside out. None can teach you, none can make you spiritual. There is no other teacher but your own soul.

11. We are what our thoughts have made us; so take care about what you think. Words are secondary. Thoughts live; they travel far.

12. The more we come out and do good to others, the more our hearts will be purified, and God will be in them.

13. All differences in this world are of degree, and not of kind, because oneness is the secret of everything.

14. Do one thing at a time, and while doing it put your whole soul into it to the exclusion of all else.

15. The greatest sin is to think that you are weak.

16. Take risks in your life. If you win, you can lead; if you lose, you can guide.

17. Anything that makes you weak, physically, intellectually, and spiritually, reject as poison.

18. The very reason for nature's existence is for the education of the soul.

19. GOD Is To Be Worshipped As The One Beloved, Dearer Than Everything In This And Next Life.

****

48. Thomas Fuller

Historian, Cleric

Nationality: English (British)

Born: June 19, 1608, in Aldwinkle St Peter, England

Death: August 16, 1661, in London, England

Age: 53

Known for his writings, including "The Worthies of England" and "A History of the Worthies of England."

1. "I was born with a glass eye. My parents didn't want me to feel left out, so they bought me a glass leg."

2. "I used to be indecisive, but now I'm not so sure."

3. "If you're not part of the solution, you're part of the precipitate."

4. "I went to the bank and asked the teller for change. She asked me, 'What kind?' I said, 'Anything. Some nickels, dimes, pennies — something I can jingle in my pocket when I walk.' She gave me a brochure for a savings account."

5. "I got a free sample of shampoo in the mail the other day. It's supposed to give you thicker hair, but I'm not sure how I can tell. I haven't had any hair for the past 20 years."

6. "I bought some shoes from a drug dealer. I don't know what he laced them with, but I've been tripping all day."

7. "I took the SAT's. I got 400 on the math section. They told me I wasn't ready for college. I said, 'I wasn't ready for high school either!'"

8. "I went to a seafood disco last night. Lots of shellfish dancing."

9. "I used to have a fear of public speaking. Now I have a fear of not having a fear of public speaking."

10. "I bought some antidepressants from a drug dealer. He said, 'Take these with milk.' I said, 'But I don't have any milk.' He said, 'Go buy some. Milk is good for your bones.' I said, 'But I don't have any bones.' He said, 'Go buy some.'"

11. "I used to work in a shoe store. Someone came in and asked for loafers. I said, 'Do you have a warrant?'"

12. "I'm on a seafood diet. I see food, and I eat it."

13. "I went to the zoo the other day. It was pretty empty. The only animal there was a dog. It was a shih tzu. I kept asking the zookeeper why it was there. He said, 'We're having a shih tzu exhibition.' I said, 'Is that an all-day thing?'"

14. "I like to do dangerous things. Like eating alphabet soup one letter at a time."

15. "I took a taxi to the library the other day. The driver asked me if I wanted to go around the block. I said, 'No, I'm just returning this book.'"

16. "I met a guy who was addicted to soap. He was clean, but he couldn't stop lathering."

17. "I went to the doctor and told him I broke my arm in two places. He told me to stop going to those places."

18. "I used to be addicted to caffeine. Then I quit cold turkey. Now I get my kicks from lukewarm Pepsi."

19. "I went to a funeral the other day. It was pretty depressing. They didn't even have any cake."

20. "I'm not sure what's wrong with my brain. I keep thinking I'm a fire engine."

21. "I used to have a fear of heights. Then I fell off a cliff. I'm cured now."

22. "Fate hangs precariously in the balance, ever shifting, now this way, now that."

****

49. Thomas Jefferson

Founding Father, U.S. President

Nationality: American

Born: April 13, 1743, in Shadwell, Virginia, USA

Death: July 4, 1826, in Charlottesville, Virginia, USA

Age: 83

Author of the Declaration of Independence and the third President of the United States.

1. "The tree of liberty must be refreshed from time to time with the blood of patriots and tyrants. It is its natural manure."

2. "A little rebellion, now and then, is a good thing. It is the medicine necessary to keep the state healthy."

3. "The care of human life and happiness and not their destruction, is the first and only legitimate object of good government."

4. "I am not a friend to a rigid adherence to forms, either in science or politics. I am glad that others pay attention to the minucia, for it facilitates my escape to the vast and magnificent whole."

5. "I tremble for my country when I reflect that God is just, that His justice cannot sleep forever."

6. "When the people fear their government, there is tyranny; when the government fears the people, there is liberty."

7. "Education is the price of liberty."

8. "The price of freedom is eternal vigilance."

9. "The legitimate powers of government extend to such acts only as are injurious to society."

10. "Those who deny freedom to others deserve it not for themselves."

11. "The natural progress of things is towards liberty."

12. "The greatest happiness which this world affords is the happiness of having friends, whom we trust, and who trust us."

13. "I have sworn upon the altar of God eternal hostility against every form of tyranny over the mind of man."

14. "Honesty is the best policy."

15. "The only freedom which deserves the name is the freedom of pursuing our own happiness."

16. "The greatest service which can be rendered to any country is to raise the standards of its citizens."

17. "Never put off for tomorrow what you can do today."

18. "A nation is a society formed for the purpose of mutual defence. Its members owe to one another, and also to the public, a reciprocal obligation of service."

19. "If at any time the people become indifferent to their rights, they deserve to be slaves."

20. "I hold that a little rebellion now and then is a good thing, as necessary in the political world as storms in the physical."

21. "Governments are instituted among men, deriving their just powers from the consent of the governed."

22. "The laws of nature are the laws of God, whose works we study in order to know His will."

23. "The natural liberty of man, to use his own faculties, to pursue his own happiness, is his birthright."

24. "The earth belongs in usufruct to the living; the dead had their usufruct while they lived."

****

50. Thomas Carlyle

Essayist, Historian

Nationality: Scottish

Born: December 4, 1795,
in Ecclefechan, Dumfriesshire, Scotland

Death: February 5, 1881, in London, England

Age: 85

Noted for his historical writings, including "The French Revolution: A History."

1. "Silence is the most perfect form of speech."

2. "A man's good fortune may change; but good principle, either in public or private affairs, never."

3. "The greatest glory in living lies not in never falling, but in rising every time we fall."

4. "Do the duty which lies nearest thee, which whoever sees it knows thou canst do, and then the second will appear; and that thou dost."

5. "No man or woman of true worth was ever truly appreciated and not calumniated by his or her contemporaries."

6. "What we achieve inwardly will change what we achieve outwardly."

7. "Blessed is the man who has found his work; let him ask no other blessedness."

8. "A peasant who respects his calling as he ought is one of the worthiest soul-objects under the sun."

9. "Silence is more eloquent than words."

10. "One thing only, remember; whatsoever thy hand findeth to do, do it with all thy might."

11. "All that a man does outwardly is but the symptom of his hidden life within."

12. "The good is the beautiful."

13. "The beginning of all worth in man is to take the first step. In the second step we climb higher, and the third will lift us to a mountain view."

14. "Doubt not, O reader, but every word of this history hath its significance."

15. "A specious, superficial excellence is the surest mark of wretchedness."

16. "Nay, the whole universe, if it be not an immense SOOTY SMOKE-cloud, what better is it!"

17. "Silence, after all, even for the wise, is wisdom."

18. "The future belongs to those who believe in the beauty of their dreams."

19. "He who has a tongue has a town."

20. "The end of man is an action, not a thought."

21. "It is not what we eat but what we digest that makes us strong."

22. "A thousand difficulties, a thousand failures, they are nothing to me, if I succeed only in one thing."

23. "The man who cannot learn, has a bad master."

24. "Show me the man who has no faults, and I will show you the one who has nothing to amend."

****

> Life is Too short for arguments. Just say "I don't care" and move on.

51. Victor Hugo

Novelist, Poet

Nationality: French

Born: February 26, 1802, in Besançon, France

Death: May 22, 1885, in Paris, France

Age: 83

Wrote "Les Misérables" and "The Hunchback of Notre-Dame."

1. "Music expresses that which cannot be said and on which it is impossible to be silent."

2. "Even the darkest night will end and the sun will rise."

3. "No one is as blind as the person who will not see."

4. "To love and be loved is to feel the sun from both sides."

5. "Laughter is the sun that drives away the winter from the human face."

6. "Life is a flower for which love is the honey."

7. "A book is the completed thought of a soul."

8. "There is nothing more powerful than an idea whose time has come."

9. "The greatest glory in living lies not in never falling, but in rising every time we fall."

10. "Misery loves company."

11. "To live without convictions is to live without dignity."

12. "He who opens a school door, closes a prison."

13. "Nothing weakens authority like allowing it to be questioned."

14. "The future has a bright side which appeals to the young, and a dark side which appeals to the old."

15. "There are certain afflictions in life that can best be borne by a smile."

16. "Destiny is not a matter of chance, it is a matter of choice."

17. "The soul should always have something of the infinite."

18. "There is one thing more painful than death: it is to be buried alive."

19. "The smallest cottage is large enough to hold happiness."

20. "Love is the sun of the soul."

21. "The supreme happiness of life is the conviction that we are loved."

22. "He who learns, but does not think, is lost. He who thinks, but does not learn, is in great danger."

23. "There is something infinitely healing in the repeated refrains of nature - the assurance that dawn comes after night, and spring after winter."

24. "One word frees us of all the weight and pain of life: That word is love."

25. "To be happy at home is the ultimate result of all ambition."

26. "A great soul is an eagle; it never loses its hold on what it seizes, and never lets go of what it grasps."

27. "The only prison that can ever bind you is fear of your own self."

28. "There is no sincerer love than the love of food."

29. "A man is not old until regrets take the place of dreams."

30. "Sleep is the death that knows no waking."

31. "The more a man meditates upon good thoughts, the more the face becomes like an angel."

32. "Patriotism is love of country. Nationalism is hatred of other countries."

33. "He who laughs, lasts."

34. "The only happiness a wise man should look for is within; without that there is none."

35. "Silence is the language of God, all else is poor translation."

36. "A mother's happiness is like a beacon, lighting up the future but reflected from the past."

37. "Every heart sings a song incomplete, until another heart whispers the missing rhyme."

38. "The bird a nest, the spider a web, man friendship."

39. "There is always a madness in love, but there is also always some reason in madness."

40. "A thousand years in your sight are but yesterday."

****

52. Virgil

Epic Poet

Nationality: Roman (Ancient Roman)

Born: October 15, 70 BC, in Andes, Cisalpine Gaul (now Italy)

Death: September 21, 19 BC, in Brundisium, Roman Empire (now Brindisi, Italy)

Age: 50

Author of the epic poems "The Aeneid" and "The Georgics."

1. "Beauty fades, but virtue blooms eternal."

2. "Silence is golden; speech is silver."

3. "The gods help those who help themselves."

4. "The course of true love never did run smooth." (adapted from Shakespeare)

5. "What hurts worse than a broken heart? Regret."

6. "The bravest thing is to know one's own ignorance."

7. "Small things often lead to great mischiefs."

8. "Time and tide wait for no man."

9. "The way to heaven is paved with good intentions."

10. "Count your blessings, not your troubles."

11. "Fortune favors the bold."

12. "All men die, not all men truly live."

13. "Speak little, listen much, and ponder all."

14. "Silence often means more than eloquence."

15. "Beware the Greeks bearing gifts." (translated quote from Aeneid)

16. "Love conquers all things." (adapted from Terence)

17. "A tear is enough to make amends for any mistake."

18. "Hope springs eternal in the human breast."

19. "A brave man is a master of fate."

20. "The greatest gift one can give is a part of oneself."

21. "Easy it is to fall into error; to escape is hard."

22. "He who knows himself, knows God."

23. "Fame's sweet reward awaits the conquering hero."

24. "The mind unburdened is as light as a feather."

****

53. Voltaire

Philosopher, Writer

Nationality: French

Born: November 21, 1694, in Paris, France

Death: May 30, 1778, in Paris, France

Age: 83

Prominent Enlightenment thinker and author of "Candide."

1. "Think for yourself and let others enjoy the privilege of doing so too."

2. "Judge a man by his questions rather than his answers."

3. "Doubt is not a pleasant condition, but certainty is absurd."

4. "I disapprove of what you say, but I will defend to the death your right to say it."

5. "To learn to think is to learn to doubt."

6. "The best is the enemy of the good."

7. "A garden is a love story, written in vegetables."

8. "Ordinary men contemplate the extraordinary; extraordinary men contemplate the ordinary."

9. "It is difficult to free fools from the chains they revere."

10. "To live is to think."

11. "The only way to deal with an unfree world is to become absolutely free yourself."

12. "The only tyrant I accept is the truth."

13. "Work spares us from three great evils: vice, boredom, and need."

14. "All animals are equal, but some animals are more equal than others." (Animal Farm reference)

15. "Candide, or Optimism," is my masterpiece. It is the ironic history of a young, gullible optimist named Candide, who journeys through the world and experiences its horrors and injustices.

16. "The best way to make the best is to make the most of what you have."

17. "Silence is the true wisdom of God; one should be silent on what one does not understand."

18. "I may not agree with you, but I will defend to the death your right to

say it."

19. "The greatest happiness which this world affords is the happiness of having friends, whom we trust, and who trust us."

20. "The more I learn, the more I doubt."

21. "The more a man meditates upon good thoughts, the more the face becomes like an angel."

22. "The sleep of reason produces monsters."

****

> The best **revenge** is to improve yourself.

54. Wayne Dyer

Self-Help Author, Motivational Speaker

Nationality: American

Born: May 10, 1940, in Detroit, Michigan, USA

Death: August 29, 2015, in Maui, Hawaii, USA

Age: 75

Prolific self-help author and motivational speaker.

1. "If you change the way you look at things, the things you look at change."

2. "You cannot always control what happens to you, but you can control your attitude towards what happens to you."

3. "There is no such thing as failure. The only real mistake is giving up."

4. "Don't dwell on mistakes. Dwell on possibilities."

5. "Don't let your past steal your present."

6. "The greatest discovery of all time is that a person can change his own future by merely changing his attitude."

7. "You'll never get ahead of anyone as long as you try to get ahead of everyone."

8. "The only person you are destined to become is the person you decide to be."

9. "Your intentions always become actions."

10. "It's not what you achieve, it's what you overcome that defines your true success."

11. "Go for it anyway. The thrill of victory makes the risk of failure worthwhile."

12. "Everything you ever wanted is on the other side of fear."

13. "What you focus on expands, and what you think on, you become."

14. "You cannot fail at something you are not willing to start."

15. "Excuses are like barnacles; they attach themselves to the bottom of your life and slow you down."

16. "You are unique and irreplaceable."

17. "The only place where success comes before work is in the dictionary."

18. "Believe in yourself and the rest of the world will fall in line."

19. "The universe doesn't owe you anything. It's up to you to create your own miracles."

20. "Gratitude is not a destination; it's a way of life."

21. "You are never too old to set another goal or to dream a new dream."

22. "The mind is everything. What you think you become."

23. "The purpose of life is to wake up."

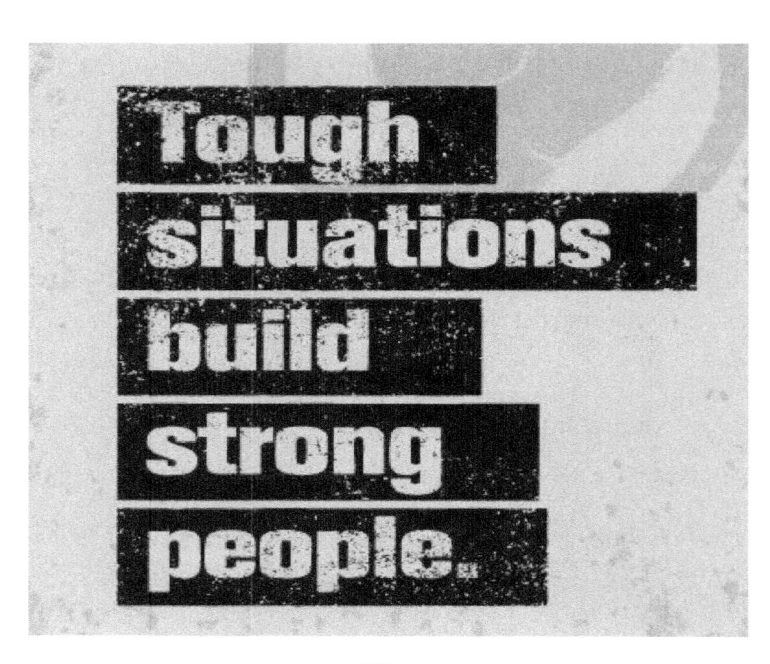

****

> **Tough situations build strong people.**

55. Will Rogers

Humorist, Actor

Nationality: American

Born: November 4, 1879, in Oologah, Indian Territory (now Oklahoma, USA)

Death: August 15, 1935, in Point Barrow, Alaska, USA (plane crash)

Age: 55

Renowned for his wit and humor in newspapers, radio, and films.

1. "The quickest way to turn a stranger into a friend is to show them you're interested in them."

2. "Never aim higher than you can shoot, but always shoot higher than you aim."

3. "The greatest thing about a new year is that it gives you 365 days to start all over again."

4. "Everything is funny as long as it happens to somebody else."

5. "Don't go around saying the world owes you a living. The world owes you nothing. It was here first."

6. "Humor is like a rubber band. The further you stretch it, the harder it comes back."

7. "I never met a man I didn't like."

8. "Good times and bad times go in circles. It's all in your mind, the way you take it."

9. "The trouble with all of us is not that we don't have brains enough, but we have too many opinions."

10. "Never criticize a thing you can't understand. The highest compliment you can pay a man is to try to understand what he is doing."

11. "If you ever find yourself in a hole, the first thing to do is stop digging."

12. "The best way to get rid of the blues is to help somebody else have theirs."

13. "We can't all succeed, but we can all try."

14. "Never take more than you can give."

15. "Never laugh when you're on fire."

16. "There's nothing as funny as truth in fiction."

17. "The only real trouble with politics is that there are more politicians than jokes."

18. "Be grateful for the present, be curious about the future, and learn from the past."

19. "Live your life so that whenever you come to a point where you're ashamed of yourself, you know you're alone."

20. "Too many of us are running around with our tongues hanging out looking for sympathy instead of looking for solutions."

21. "Don't let yesterday take up too much of your today."

22. "If you want to be remembered, write songs or books; if you want to be forgotten, give a speech."

23. "Every time you take a stand, you put your butt on the line."

****

DO IT TODAY OR REGRET IT TOMORROW

56. William Hazlitt

Essayist, Critic

Nationality: English (British)

Born: April 10, 1778, in Maidstone, England

Death: September 18, 1830, in Soho, London, England

Age: 52

Prominent essayist and critic known for his literary and philosophical writings.

1. "The only secret of success in society is to find out what a man wants and help him to get it."

2. "The knowledge of good and evil is a knowledge of pleasure and pain. Those who have had the most pleasure must have the most pain."

3. "The art of conversation is the art of the heart; it is to give, and to receive, pleasure."

4. "The soul of poetry is the element of wonder."

5. "The greatest good is what we least know."

6. "The future belongs to those who believe in the beauty of their dreams."

7. "There is but one truly aristocratic occupation – that of thinking."

8. "The art of living is the art of making good use of bad weather."

9. "The more a man meditates upon good thoughts, the more the face becomes like an angel."

10. "What happens once, may never happen again; but what has happened twice, may very probably happen again."

11. "The strongest and sweetest songs yet remain to be sung."

12. "The greatest happiness this world affords is the happiness of having friends, whom we trust, and who trust us."

13. "It is only the fanatic who is always certain."

14. "The only infallible cure for vanity is death."

15. "A laugh is worth a hundred groans in any market."

16. "Hope is the chief blessing, memory the chief curse."

17. "Man is born an optimist, and dies a pessimist."

18. "The heart may cease to beat, but the memory of its affections lasts forever."

19. "All the world's a stage, and all the men and women merely players." (Paraphrasing Shakespeare)

20. "The more I learn, the more I doubt."

21. "The tongue is a fire, a world of iniquity: so is the tongue among our members, that it defileth the whole body, and setteth on fire the course of nature; and it is set on fire of hell."

22. "There is no such thing as a beautiful woman; but if there were, she would not be a woman."

23. "The greater the difficulty, the more glory in surmounting it."

24. "There is nothing worse than a friend who is also an enemy."

****

THERE IS NO SUCCESS WITHOUT PAIN AND STRUGGLE.

57. William James

Philosopher, Psychologist

Nationality: Ancient Greek

Born: January 11, 1842, in New York City, New York, USA

Death: August 26, 1910, in Chocorua, New Hampshire, USA

Age: 68

Pragmatist philosopher and author of "The Varieties of Religious Experience."

1. "The greatest discovery of my generation is that a human being can alter his life by altering his attitudes."

2. "Act as if what you do makes a difference. It does."

3. "The greatest enemy of any flower is the shadow of the flower that has bloomed before it."

4. "The function of philosophy is to free us from the fear of things."

5. "The only person you are destined to become is the person you decide to be."

6. "Change your thinking, change your life."

7. "The greatest gift you can give to anyone is your attention."

8. "Believe that you can and you're halfway there."

9. "Our greatest weakness lies in giving up. The most certain way to succeed is always to try just one more time."

10. "The art of living well is the art of making a good adjustment to the reality of things — to reality, not to your own longings, demands, desires, or wishes."

11. "Man is not a creature of circumstances, but a creature who can create circumstances."

12. "The greatest remedy for those who are afraid, lonely or unhappy is to go outside, somewhere where they can be quite alone with the heavens, nature and God. Find God in nature, and you will find peace in your soul."

13. "The greatest thing in this world is not so much to find yourself as to create yourself."

14. "The pragmatic test of truth is what works."

15. "Don't live in the past, don't worry about the future, focus on the present moment."

16. "The habit of attention is the root of all voluntary action."

17. "The greatest use of life is to spend it on something that will outlast it."

18. "The difference between a successful person and others is not a lack of strength, not a lack of knowledge, but rather a lack of will."

19. "Education is the preparation for life; education is life itself."

20. "The greatest compliment that was ever paid to me was when someone asked me what I thought, and attended to my answer."

21. "The deepest craving of human nature is the need to be appreciated."

22. "The price of greatness is responsibility."

23. "The only thing that stands between you and your dream is the will to try and the belief that it is actually possible."

24. "The greatest glory in living lies not in never falling, but in rising every time we fall."

****

58. William Shakespeare

Playwright, Poet

Nationality: English (British)

Born: Baptized on April 26, 1564, in Stratford-upon-Avon, England

Death: April 23, 1616, in Stratford-upon-Avon, England

Age: 52 (Approx.)

Considered one of the greatest playwrights in history, known for his plays and sonnets.

1. "To be or not to be, that is the question." (Hamlet)

2. "Parting is such sweet sorrow." (Romeo and Juliet)

3. "The fault, dear Brutus, is not in our stars, but in ourselves, that we are underlings." (Julius Caesar)

4. "All the world's a stage, and all the men and women merely players." (As You Like It)

5. "Brevity is the soul of wit." (Hamlet)

6. "What a piece of work is a man! How noble in reason, how infinite in faculty! In form and moving how express and admirable! In action how like an angel, in apprehension how like a god! The beauty of the world, the paragon of animals—and yet, to me, what is this

quintessence of dust?" (Hamlet)

7. "Love all, trust a few, do wrong to none." (All's Well That Ends Well)

8. "Cowards die many times before their deaths; The valiant never taste of death but once." (Julius Caesar)

9. "The course of true love never did run smooth." (A Midsummer Night's Dream)

10. "Friends, Romans, countrymen, lend me your ears!" (Julius Caesar)

11. "There are more things in heaven and earth, Horatio, than are dreamt of in your philosophy." (Hamlet)

12. "Some are born great, some achieve greatness, and some have greatness thrust upon them." (Twelfth Night)

13. "The fool doth think he is wise, but the wise man knows himself to be a fool." (As You Like It)

14. "Hell is empty, and all the devils are here." (The Tempest)

15. "What's done is done." (Macbeth)

16. "The evil that men do lives after them; The good is oft interred with their bones." (Julius Caesar)

17. "To thine own self be true." (Hamlet)

18. "Though this be madness, yet there is method in it." (Hamlet)

19. "It is a tale told by an idiot, full of sound and fury, signifying nothing." (Macbeth)

20. "The time is out of joint. O cursed spite, That ever I was born to set it right!" (Hamlet)

21. "Out, damned spot!" (Macbeth)

22. "There is a tide in the affairs of men, Which, taken at the flood, leads on to fortune; Omitted, all the voyage of their life Is bound in shallows and miseries. And we must take the current when it serves, Or lose our ventures." (Julius Caesar)

23. "Suspicion always haunts the guilty mind." (Richard III)

24. "One good deed dying tongueless sleepeth not in the dust." (All's Well That Ends Well)

25. "And oftentimes, to win us to our harm, The instruments of darkness tell us truths." (Macbeth)

****

59. Winston Churchill

British Prime Minister, Statesman

Nationality: English (British)

Born: November 30, 1874, in Blenheim Palace, England

Death: January 24, 1965, in London, England

Age: 90

Led Britain during World War II and known for his powerful speeches.

1. "Success consists of going from failure to failure without loss of enthusiasm."

2. "The greatest glory in living lies not in never falling, but in rising every time we fall."

3. "The pessimist sees the difficulty in every opportunity. The optimist sees the opportunity in every difficulty."

4. "Never give in, never give in, never, never, in nothing, great or small, large or petty - never give in except to convictions of honour and good sense."

5. "A pessimist is someone who looks at a half-full glass and sees it as half-empty. An optimist sees it as half-full, and the engineer sees a glass that is twice the size it needs to be."

6. "A lie gets halfway around the world before the truth has put on its shoes."

7. "The weak can never forgive. Forgiveness is the attribute of the strong."

8. "Difficulties mastered are opportunities won."

9. "You can't eat glory, but it's a wonderful sauce to the cabbage of life."

10. "The farther backward you can look, the farther forward you are likely to see."

11. "The future belongs to those who believe in the beauty of their dreams."

12. "Continuous effort - not strength or intelligence - is the key to unlocking our potential."

13. "Action speaks louder than words, but not nearly so often."

14. "I am an optimist. It does not seem very reasonable, but I have not found any other way of being happy."

15. "A good laugh and a long sleep are the two best cures for anything."

16. "The best time to start a thing is now. The second best time is tomorrow."

17. "The only limit to our realization of tomorrow will be our doubts of today."

18. "Never be afraid to try something new. Remember, amateurs built the ark, professionals built the Titanic."

19. "The best reason to smile is because you're alive. You have survived everything that has tried to kill you so far."

20. "Twenty years from now you will be more disappointed by the things that you didn't do than by the ones you did do. So throw off the bowlines, sail away from safe harbor, catch the trade winds in your sails. Explore. Dream. Discover."

21. "You miss 100% of the shots you don't take."

22. "Man is not made for defeat. A man can be destroyed but not defeated."

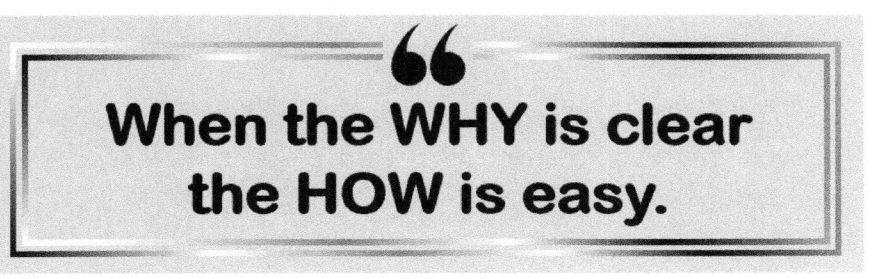

****

> **When the WHY is clear the HOW is easy.**

60. Zig Ziglar

Motivational Speaker, Author

Nationality: American

Born: November 6, 1926,
in Coffee County, Alabama, USA

Death: November 28, 2012,
in Plano, Texas, USA

Age: 86

Known as Hilary Hinton Ziglar. Highly influential motivational speaker and author, known for inspiring personal development and success.

1. "What you get by achieving one goal is not as important as what you become by achieving it."

2. "A goal is a dream with a deadline."

3. "If you can dream it, you can achieve it."

4. "The only place success comes before work is in the dictionary."

5. "You cannot fail at something you are not willing to start."

6. "It's your reaction to adversity, not adversity itself, that determines your destiny."

7. "People often say that motivation doesn't last. Well, neither does bathing - that's why we need to do it daily."

8. "Fear is a liar. It will tell you that you can't do it. You CAN do it."

9. "A positive attitude causes a chain reaction of positive thoughts, events, and outcomes. It is a catalyst that creates a ripple effect of positivity that can change the world."

10. "The greatest mistake you can make in life is to be afraid to make one."

11. "Don't let yesterday take up too much of your today."

12. "You're born to win, but you have to plan to win, prepare to win, and then expect to win."

13. "Happiness is not something you achieve, it's a result of how you choose to live."

14. "If you believe in yourself and have the courage to chase your dreams, anything is possible."

15. "Help others achieve their dreams and yours will come true."

16. "You have everything you need to achieve your goals."

17. "Failure is only temporary. Never give up on your dreams."

18. "The mind is everything. What you think you become."

19. "The only person you are destined to become is the person you decide to be."

20. "A smile is the universal language of kindness."

21. "There are two days in the year that you cannot do anything: yesterday and tomorrow."

22. "The key to success is to focus on what you control, not what you don't."

23. "The past is history. The future is a mystery. Today is a gift. That's why it's called the present."

24. "You cannot always control the circumstances, but you can always control your attitude."

****

> **IF YOUR HABITS DON'T CHANGE, YOU DON'T HAVE NEW YEAR. YOU JUST HAVE ANOTHER YEAR.**

HELP THE WORLD TO GET MOTIVATED AND INSPIRED

I'd appreciate if you could share your book review & rating to help people to find and get the book. All suggestions are welcome! Scan the QR code to direct to book page on Amazon.

Amazon Review Page:

USA

UK

CANADA

AUSTRALIA

For Other Amazon Marketplaces,
Search by ASIN: **B0CL7XNBZW**

👉 Chekout out new books series "Quotes for life" – A series of 8 books, categorised to address specifc topics

All 8 Books detail content -

1	Self Development	Improvement, Communcation, Efficiency, Integrity, Patience, Confidance, Performance, Consistency
2	Health	Body, Fitness, Meditation, Exercise, Diet, Mental Health, Medicines, Holistic Healing, Wellness
3	Positivity	Breakup, Depression/Anxiety, Hearthbreak, Failure, Weakness, Rejection, Negativity, Disability, Fear, Ego.
4	Relationship	Friends, Family, Relationship, Emotions, Mom/Dad, Brother/Sister, Husband/Wife, Trust, Love, Care
5	Work	Productivity, Success, Challenges, Innovation, Quality, Team work, Leadership, Oppertunities, Goal, Planning
6	Business	Investments, Sales/Marketing, Profit/Loss, Money, Risk
7	Spiritual	Karma, Faith, Fate, Death, Hope, Time, Luck, Destiny, Mind, Nature.
8	Religion	Geeta, Bible, Quaran, Buddha, Religion, Self, God

Printed in Great Britain
by Amazon